GUIDELINES
FOR
EFFECTIVE
RESEARCH TO PUBLICATION:
A CONCISE APPROACH

Second Edition

Paulchris Okpala.
D.HSc, MHA, MPA, RCP, CRT

STRATTON PRESS
We Celebrate Your Story

GUIDELINES FOR EFFECTIVE RESEARCH TO PUBLICATION
Copyright © 2022 **Paulchris Okpala. D.HSc, MHA, MPA, RCP, CRT**

Stratton Press Publishing
831 N Tatnall Street Suite M #188,
Wilmington, DE 19801
www.stratton-press.com
1-888-323-7009

ISBN (Paperback): 978-1-64895-955-4
ISBN (Ebook): 978-1-64895-956-1

Printed in the United States of America

CONTENTS

Part 2.
Basic Guidelines on Journal Selection:
The Packaging of the Research Material to a Manuscript

PREFACE

W riting a book on performing superior research from beginning to end requires an author with vast experience conducting research and publishing papers.

I consider myself fortunately blessed to have had the opportunity to finish various research projects successfully. As a consequence, I have over thirty peer-reviewed scientific articles in a variety of journals.

Additionally, I developed and taught a variety of research approaches to graduate and undergraduate students.

I started this book with the intention of sharing my experiences as a researcher and full-time professor. Each of the research approaches I used and each of the pieces I published presented distinct issues worth debating.

I am cognizant of the obstacles encountered by novice researchers and students embarking on their first venture into scientific inquiry. I am aware of the anxiety, disappointment, and stress that accompany submission rejection and the ramifications for academic achievement.

I also understand students' struggles with balancing research duties and other academic obligations. As a consequence of these experiences, I've always wished to provide new researchers and students with a more straightforward book that teaches them how to properly arrange their work and write publishable papers. As such, I want to help novice researchers and students effectively conceive and conduct research, as well as publish high-quality publications by addressing technical concerns that may result in manuscript rejection.

I spent almost a year writing this book. The procedure started with the collection of personal notes and information from my notebook. I spent the first part of the year combing through my research files—both accepted and rejected manuscripts.

Additionally, I examined my interactions with editors and reviewers. I had conversations with my colleagues in the second quarter of the year about their struggles in their early years of research.

I also discussed the major areas of focus for writing high-quality work that would be accepted by a journal. I engaged students throughout the writing process, aiming to get a greater understanding of the current challenges they face.

The purpose of this book is to teach students and young researchers how to conduct productive research and write publishable papers. The book's first portion covers the qualities of high-quality research. Following that, the book provides concise directions for creating publishable research by identifying the fundamental characteristics of a title and the many strategies used to create it.

The book addresses the issue statement and the qualities of a well-phrased problem statement. Additionally, the book addresses how to develop a compelling research topic and how to avoid common research mistakes.

Key components of conceptual and theoretical frameworks are explored, as well as the criteria, that should be used by researchers when building conceptual and theoretical frameworks.

Finally, the literature review, methodology, results explanation, and abstract are all detailed.

The first half of the book concludes with a checklist for assessing the chapter's individual components. The second half of the book includes advice for selecting and packaging manuscripts. It details when and how to choose the appropriate journal.

Additionally, it details the steps that should be taken to guarantee that writing is clear, pertinent, and plagiarism-free.

Additionally, I discuss how to communicate with editors with an emphasis on how to manage submission rejections.

Finally, the article explores how researchers might efficiently manage their time.

I would advise researchers who want to utilize this information as a guide for their studies to begin by reading chapter 12 on time-saving strategies. The chapter teaches researchers how to organize their work in such a way that their publications are successfully submitted on time.

Following the completion of the preceding eight chapters, the reader may proceed to chapter 9. Chapter 9 enables readers to choose a journal and read the publication's instructions, which give further help on developing the methods, publishing the results, and providing the discussion.

ACKNOWLEDGMENTS

My appreciation goes to God Almighty, whose boundless compassion and grace enabled me to successfully collect sufficient resources to write this book. Furthermore, I am grateful to my devoted wife, Frances Chinonso Okpala, BSc, MSc, who read this book with attention and made insightful suggestions on improving the flow of information.

Additionally, I am grateful to my children—Vanessa Somtochukwu Okpala (eighth grade), Bryan Chiemelie Okpala (fifth grade), Nicole Ifunanya Okpala (third grade), and Jason Chimaobim Okpala (second grade)—for understanding the importance of working on this book by providing me with the time and space necessary to complete it successfully and comfortably.

PART 1

Basic Guidelines for the Development of Publishable Research

CHAPTER 1

Selection of the Title

The title of your study serves as the article's core argument. It is the first portion of the article that the editor and reviewers will evaluate before reading the abstract and body of the text (Bavdekar 2016). As a result, it is critical to give an intriguing and informative title that piques the reader's interest.

Huston and Choi (2017) assert that the title should serve as a hook enticing people to read the content.

While this book starts with a chapter on title development, the reader should realize that the ultimate title will be selected when the study is complete (Bavdekar 2016).

It is recommended that the researcher begin the study with a working title to serve as a guide and ensure that the research subject does not get lost in the shuffle.

As a result, rather than extending the title's evolution over many chapters, I condensed the information into a single chapter.

This chapter demonstrates how to create an article title that appropriately represents the article's content. Additionally, this chapter addresses the following factors that affect how titles are created:

- A discussion of the many types of titles
- Creating a provisional title
- Suggestions for writing a research title that is effective
- Instructions for writing a title
- Checklist for determining if a title is successful

What Type of Title Fits Your Research?

Although there are up to thirteen distinct titles, this book will focus on three major categories (Hartley 2012).

The first kind is the declarative title, which is comprised of the research results or conclusions. A declarative title is created after the study is completed (Bavdekar 2016).

The second sort of title is the descriptive title, which provides a succinct summary of the study without revealing the results or conclusions.

In a descriptive title, the study is described by mentioning the significant components of the research topic. A descriptive title provides readers with comprehensive information about the study, increasing the visibility of the manuscript (Habibzadeh and Yadollahie 2010; Kumar 2013).

Finally, the third form of title is the interrogative, which restates the research question.

Developing a Working Title

Although the title is often produced last, the working title is critical in ensuring the researcher keeps and can restore focus after the end of the investigation (Bavdekar 2016).

Writing the working title might be a demanding task for students and beginner researchers. One way to simplify the procedure is by implementing Saah and Osei's decision cycle method (2010).

This technique begins with identifying the topic, which entails describing the study's subject within the context of the more extensive program or area of interest.

The second phase is to develop the topic, which may be accomplished via tree diagrams and concept maps.

The third phase is to establish the theories and key phrases that will be used to describe the chosen subject and area.

A brief narrative is then produced regarding the facts provided above and from the narrative followed by developing a working title (Habibzadeh and Yadollahie 2010). Because the working narrative will influence the research and the study's conclusion will guide the creation of the final title, the technique is considered cyclical (Saah and Osei 2010).

Recommendations for Writing a Good Research Title

First Recommendation: A good title should communicate adequate relevant information but still be concise

A simple search on search engines such as Google Scholar will disclose that your topic of interest has multiple published papers. As a result, readers are presented with several alternatives and will often depend on the headline when deciding which article to open and read (Bavdekar 2016).

Readers are more inclined to pick the most revealing titles since their relevance and appropriateness may be clearly determined. However, since it is necessary to strike a balance between presenting as much important information as possible and being succinct (Kumar 2013), researchers should take the time to comprehend and craft a title that concisely describes the whole work in a few words (typically no more than fifteen) (Habibzadeh and Yadollahie 2010).

Second Recommendation: Identify and employ the use of key words

The use of key words in the title not only makes it more appealing but also enhances the likelihood that the paper will be picked up by literature-scanning services, thus increasing your article's exposure (Kumar 2013).

Key words can be found within your research topic—in encyclopedias used for background research or in bibliographies at the end of papers and abstracts, such as those found in APA-style publications.

Key words can also be generated using one of the many free key word generators available (Habibzadeh and Yadollahie 2010). After selecting the key words, the following step is to ensure that they are placed in a way that makes the terms the title's main point. It is recommended to place the key words at the beginning of the title.

The following are examples of excellent and terrible titles depending on the key word placement:

> *Not preferred:* Effects of Technology Adoption on the Cost of Health Care Services
> *Preferred:* Technology Adoption Reduces the Cost of Health Care Services

At times, including key words at the beginning of the title might be inconvenient and detract from the title's flow.

This difficulty may be overcome by separating the first portion, which includes the key word, from the second, which provides the explanation.

Separate the key word area from the explanation section using abbreviations such as a colon or a dash. Here is an example of how to utilize a colon in the title formulation process: "Power Dynamics between Nurses and Physicians: Identifying Pathways to Improved Health Care Delivery."

Third Recommendation: Choose how to frame the title

The title might be written in the form of a noun phrase, a statement, or a question.

The noun phrase title is the conventional style of title, consisting of a group of phrases plus a head noun.

The noun phrase title is often brief and informative and is distinguished by the inclusion of the key word at the start.

However, the usage of noun phrase titles may sometimes result in excessive generalization, leaving readers with unresolved issues (Kumar 2013). Example of a noun phrase title is "Suppression of Cancer Progression."

The benefits of framing the title as a statement outweigh the disadvantages of the noun phrase method. The inclusion of a subject and a verb in the title of a statement identifies it as a statement title. The names of statements often include additional information regarding the study's findings (Habibzadeh and Yadollahie 2010).

However, statement titles are appropriate for papers that address a particular subject and provide a straightforward solution. This is an example of a statement title: "Technology Adoption Reduces the Cost of Health Care Services."

In cases when the study issue does not have a straightforward response, the title might be structured as a question. However, the choice of framing strategy should be guided by the journal's criteria.

The author should first study the journal's requirements and review samples of previously published works (Habibzadeh and Yadollahie 2010).

Fourth Recommendation: Be specific in noun phrases

When employing noun phrases, students and beginner researchers should avoid ambiguity. The usage of a string of nouns and adjectives in a title might create several alternative interpretations, which can be perplexing for readers.

Restricting noun phrases to a limit of three words and clarifying the meaning of nouns with a preposition may improve intelligibility. The two examples below illustrate a title that is unclear (example 1) and one that is clearer (example 2).

Example 1: Throat Cancer Progression Suppression
Example 2: Suppression of Cancer Progression

Procedures for Developing a Title

Following the completion of the entire manuscript, the final title is written.

The first step is to create a brief summary paragraph for the text. The second stage is to create working titles composed of phrases using the key words. The third phase is to condense the sentences by removing duplication, improving their clarity, and boosting their readability. Finally, the third phase is making the title memorable through the use of a controversial remark, a new acronym, or a famous quotation (Bavdekar 2016).

Checklist for the Assessment of an Effective Title

Table 1 provides a checklist for developing the appropriate manuscript title.

Table 1

Checklist for Developing an Appropriate Manuscript Title

Checklist item	Description
Have you adhered to the instructions provided by the journal?	Verify the maximum word count. Verify the permitted characters, the suggested structure, and the components.
Is the main theme captured?	The title should clearly state the purpose of the investigation.
Is it clear?	The title should be concise with no room for interpretational ambiguity or uncertainty.
Is it of the appropriate length?	The title should be long enough to include all the essential components without excluding anything.
Are the key words captured?	Key words are required to enhance visibility and discoverability.
Is it attractive and catchy?	The reader's interest is piqued by the author's deft use of language.
Does it have technical words?	Ascertain that the title is readily understandable to the intended audience.
Does it have the results of the study?	If it is included, it should be inspiring and unquestionable.

CHAPTER 2

Formulation of the
Problem Statement

A poorly phrased and ineffective problem statement is one of the writing shortcomings that finally results in the submission of low-quality papers. Students and rookie researchers must recognize that the problem statement is the core of the study and requires careful formulation (Flamez, Lenz, Balkin, and Smith 2017).

Apart from the title and abstract, the problem statement is the first component of a research paper that the assessors and readers pay close attention to and scrutinize. The problem statement emphasizes the study's advantages and provides a framework for comprehending the research (Flamez et al. 2017). The issue statement explains why the study is being conducted.

In research, a phenomenon qualifies as a problem requiring a solution, and there are several alternative solutions (Wentz 2013). In an academic setting where students have a certain amount of time to conduct their studies (Flamez et al. 2017), students and budding researchers must recognize that circumstances (issues) without a solution are not worth their attention.

For instance, although analyzing the meaning of time is a current issue, is it worthwhile for a physics student to pursue this as a study topic? Perhaps not. Then an example of an issue that may need a solution but does not seem to have one is the problem of death. As a result, students who investigate how individuals may attain immortality will find that it makes no sense, at least not in our current view of reality.

Students must grasp how to structure a problem statement to result in quantifiable research questions that can be investigated using the correct scientific technique.

This section discusses how to develop an effective problem statement and avoid common problems while writing it. This chapter discusses the following components of the statement's problem:

i. Definition of the term
ii. Importance of the problem statement
iii. Characteristics of a well-framed problem statement
iv. Materials required for problem statement formulation
v. Checklist for evaluating an effective problem statement

What Is a Problem Statement?

As already hinted in the introduction to this section, the term *problem statement*, as used in research, refers to the existing situation that needs to be assessed to identify the appropriate solution (Wentz 2013). The problem statement is basically one sentence that specifically identifies the issues that needs to be addressed (Flamez et al. 2017). However, for the problem statement to be complete, the issue stated in that one sentence needs to be qualified using several sentences and sometimes paragraphs (Wentz 2013).

Why Is the Problem Statement Important?

A well-framed problem statement is critical because it communicates the significance of the study and engages the reader (Dine, McGaghie, Bordage, and Shea 2015). By including a well-written problem statement in your work, readers may quickly grasp the context of your study without having to read the complete literature review or the supporting arguments in the background section (Flamez et al. 2017).

Additionally, readers are given the option to identify the research topics that your study is attempting to answer. A well-framed problem statement also informs the reader of the study's contribution to the body of knowledge.

Finally, the problem description introduces the study questions, hypotheses, and/or assumptions (Flamez et al. 2017).

What Are the Features of a Well-Framed Problem Statement?

There are three main features of a well-written problem statement. Each of the features is described below.

- *The problem.* As implied by the name and description, students must identify the unique problem, issue, or situation being evaluated. Typically, the problem is presented in the first paragraph's first phrase.

- *Context.* The word *context* refers to the background or literature that gives convincing justification for the stated problem's relevance.

  Contextualizing the issue and locating it within the study's current literature is critical for demonstrating how the answers to the stated problem will contribute new information to the existing body of knowledge.

Further, the context establishes the population of interest. Additionally, the issue statement contains words that describe the location of the problem (The setting; Dine et al. 2015).

- *Purpose/Research questions/statements of the objectives.* The problem statement also needs to incorporate the sentences that highlight the purpose of research. A good problem statement also provides the scope of the study.

- *Methods/Research approach.* A well-written problem statement should indicate the method that will be used to resolve the given problem. The variables (for quantitative investigations) and data sources are two parts of the approach specified in the issue description.

The problem statement's approach and methods are often articulated as a claim, which allows for future elaboration as the investigation advances (Flamez et al. 2017).

What Material Is Needed to Formulate a Problem Statement?

To write an effective problem statement, researchers must have a firm grasp of the relevant literature and the current gap in the literature (Wentz 2013). However, before diving into the literature evaluation, it is necessary to define the research topic. Thus, before developing the problem statement, students are advised to do a comprehensive study in the area of interest (Flamez et al. 2017).

Several aspects of the literature review to which students should pay close attention while writing the issue statement include findings from earlier researchers that were not completely investigated but were relevant to the selected research topic.

Personal experiences, particularly when undertaking qualitative research, contribute to the formulation of the problem statement as well.

Checklist for the Assessment of an Effective Problem Statement

Table 2 provides a checklist for the evaluation of the appropriate statement of the problem.

Table 2

Checklist for the Evaluation of the Appropriate Statement of the Problem

Item	Description
Is the problem identified?	This should be in the first sentence.
Is the problem evidence-based?	The evidence should be supported by recent literature.
Is the methodological approach identified?	The research design and paradigm needed to address the problem should be highlighted.
Is the context and population of interest described?	The population affected by the problem should be mentioned along with the geographic area.
Is the gap in literature identified appropriately?	The gap in the literature should be used to explain the importance of the problem and why it needs to be addressed.

CHAPTER 3

Formulation of the Research Question

The choice of a research question is a critical first step in developing a high-quality article that complies with the journal's standards, tackles a topic of interest to the intended audience, and adds value to the existing literature. The research question must be precise and well-articulated so that there is no ambiguity in the reader's mind about what the researcher is seeking to learn.

A researcher must determine what particular problems the work is attempting to solve or what state the study is attempting to improve. Because the research question establishes the study's relevance to the journal and subject of interest, researchers must be well-prepared with the abilities necessary to develop relevant, engaging, and researchable research questions.

This section aims to provide beginner researchers and students with the knowledge and skills necessary to craft a compelling research question. This section discusses the following components of research question formulation:

i.   When to develop the research question
ii.   What to consider when developing a research question

iii. Common errors in the formulation of the research question
iv. Research question and the research design
v. Checklist for the assessment of an effective research question

Types of Research Questions

The research question may be declarative or interrogative. A declarative research question is a statement that expresses the study's goal. The interrogative research question is phrased in such a way that it identifies a knowledge gap in the field of study.

When to Develop the Research Question

The whole study is geared toward answering the research question. As a result, it is best to begin with the research question before moving on to the other elements.

Because the research question dictates the relevant literature to be read, it must be developed before being reviewed (Churchill and Sanders 2007). Additionally, researchers must formulate a research topic first and then choose the research design necessary to answer the research question.

However, since developing the research topic is iterative, the student may need to return and reassess the research question as the study develops. The iterative approach assures the formulation of a research topic that is relevant, precise, and answerable.

What to Consider When Developing a Research Question

This section discusses the questions that students should ask themselves before deciding on a research topic.

What Is the Motivation for the Research?

The researcher must have a firm grasp on what motivates them to do the study. Is it a combination of personal and professional experiences or academic requirements?

What Do I Want to Know? What Is Known Already?

Establishing your knowledge of the subject is critical for developing the research question. The researcher must conduct a rigorous examination of the relevant literature to detect gaps (Churchill and Sanders 2007).

The gaps are then depicted as the absence of the proposed solution(s). This implies that you must use circular reasoning for each question you want to ask. You should already have some assumptions about the research question's major components. Consider the sample research question: *What is the impact of technological adoption in the cost of health care services?*

There are two assumptions in this research question:

1. There is technological adoption in the health care.
2. Technological adoption can influence the cost of health care services.

The assumptions embedded in the research question should be evidence-based.

Determining what others have done in the area of interest helps prevent attempts to reinvent the wheel, which is common among enthusiastic novice researchers.

Reviewing what others have done can make the work of researchers less tedious and more valuable because it enables one to narrow the research question to the existing gaps in literature (Churchill and Sanders 2007). Knowing what has been done also ensures that the question that is posed maximizes the participants' time and the researcher's resources by engaging in worthwhile research.

Do You Have the Time?

Asking whether you have sufficient time and resources requires the researcher to examine the time and the resources that will be required to collect, manage, and analyze the data to address the question adequately.

Do You Have the Required Expertise?

The research question determines the research design, data collection approach, and the type of analysis to be undertaken. It is therefore advisable for researchers to choose research questions they have the intellectual and technical capacity to answer.

Is It Possible to Obtain the Data?

Collecting the facts necessary to answer the question is critical. Researchers should be cautious when posing questions requiring data collection on contentious or sensitive conduct.

Further, researchers must exercise caution when formulating questions that may necessitate data collection from individuals who lack the motivation to engage or lack confidence in the researcher's study process. Additionally, researchers must avoid formulating queries that require data collection from unreachable people (Churchill and Sanders 2007). Additionally, it is prudent to prevent inquiries involving classified data acquisition or raise ethical concerns about the data collection method.

Where Should Research Questions Be Placed?

The research question should be mentioned in the abstract and introduction, and it is sometimes identified in the title, which helps the readers to discern the potential relevance of the manuscript to their area of interest.

Common Errors in the Formulation of the Research Question

Various errors prevent students and novice researchers from formulating an effective research question. Some of the common errors, as provided in table 3, include those discussed in this section.

• *Lack of specificity.* One commonly committed error is posing the research question in broad terms so that the researcher indicates the topic instead of the specific problem (Churchill and Sanders 2007).

In the example provided in table 3, it is not obvious what is going to be explored: the nature of power dynamics (how power is shared in health care teams), the effect of power dynamics on a team's performance of the team, or how the members of health care teams view power dynamics.

The corrected research question helps specify the research problem and directs the readers and the study toward a specific issue (factors influencing power dynamics) within the broad topic of power dynamics in health care teams.

- *Lack of sense.* Some research questions do not add any value to existing knowledge, and it, therefore, makes no sense investigating them.

- *Being trivial.* Another issue that students often face is stating a frivolous research question.

  According to the third example (problem 3) of an ineffective research question in table 3, researchers are limited to a yes-or-no response, which is too simplistic and gives inadequate information on the investigated topic.

Table 3

Common Problems when Developing an Effective Research Question

	Ineffective Research Question	Problems	Corrected Research Question
Problem 1	Power dynamics in health care teams	Identification of the topic (area), not the research problem	What factors influence power dynamics in inter-professional health care teams?
Problem 2	Does healthy eating improve overall health?	The research problem is not of value or does not make sense	How does food portion affect the influence of healthy eating On overall health?

Problem 3	Are ethicist consultants good communicators?	The research problem is trivial or too simple	What communication tools do ethicist consultants use? What factors affect communication among ethicist consultants? How does communication among ethicist consultants affect the client's satisfaction?

Research Question and the Research Design

The research question differs depending on the qualitative or quantitative research approach. Thus, the researcher must ensure that the research question and the research design are congruent (Churchill and Sanders 2007).

The following questions should be asked when determining the optimal research design to solve the research question: Which kinds of data are required to address the research question? Who are the participants? How will the data be gathered? How is the data going to be analyzed?

Framing Research Questions for Qualitative Studies

For qualitative designs, interrogative research questions are mainly used where the questions take the form of "What is this?" Or "What is happening here?" These designs are more concerned with the process rather than the outcome (Agee 2009).

When framing the qualitative research question, students need to understand the phenomenon, issue, or event they want to know more about. They should then choose the key words or phrases that will help them focus on their phenomenon. The key words that can be used include *construct, interpret, understand, negotiate, perceive,* and *explore* (Churchill and Sanders 2007).

When designing the research question for qualitative research, it is also important to identify the actors (the target population), the setting, and the phenomenon of interest. Look at the following example of a qualitative research question: *How do students in institutions of higher learning perceive racial discrimination?*

In this example, students represent the people (actors), an institution of higher learning is the setting, and racial discrimination is the phenomenon. The term *perceive* is used as the key word (Agee 2009).

Framing Research Questions for Quantitative Studies

A quantitative research question restates the topic of interest in operational terms to allow the gathering of empirical data used to test an already-stated hypothesis.

For quantitative research questions, students need to have a good understanding of various concepts, such as a unit of analysis, variable, and attributes (Churchill and Sanders 2007).

The *unit of analysis* refers to objects or events that are being counted or measured. In a survey, people represent the unit of analysis.

A *variable* is a concept that measurably describes a phenomenon. The variable can either be dependent (dv), a concept that is acted upon by another variable; independent (iv), one that acts upon the other variable(s); or mediating, one that influences the relationship between the dependent and independent variables.

Attributes are the categories within variables, such as male and female attributes for the variable gender.

The hypothesis is logically linked to the research question and states the relationship between variables.

With a quantitative research question, the hypothesis should be tested by gathering empirical data, which requires the use of measurable variables. The description of how the hypothesis influences the development of the research question is described in table 4.

Table 4

Framing a Quantitative Research Question Guided by the Hypothesis

| | Hypothesis Formulation | | | | |
	Step 1	Step 2	Step 3	Step 4	Step 5
Description	Initial research ques-tion: Is variable 1 related to variable 2?	Identification of iv	Identification of the direc-tion of the relationship	Phrasing the hypothesis to answer the research question and making a testable prediction	Feedback on the research question Reformulation of the research question
Example	Is the cost of health care related to the adoption of tech-nology?	Adoption of technology is the IV and therefore comes first.	Increased adoption of technology is likely to decrease the cost of health care.	The greater the adoption of technology, the higher the reduction in the cost of health care.	Are health care institutions with increased adoption of technology likely to charge less for health care services?

A summary of the possible research questions and the appropriate research designs are provided in table 5.

Table 5

Selected Research Questions and Associated Research Designs

Research Question	Research Design
Seeks people's responses to the already-stated questions	Survey
Seeks people's account of their experiences when the researcher is not sure what is important	Open-ended interview
Seeks people's real-time account and detailed description of events as they occurred	Diary study
Seeks participants' behavior in their natural setting	Observation

Checklist for the Assessment of an Effective Research Question

Table 6 provides a checklist for a good research question.

Table 6

Checklist for a Good Research Question

Item	Description
Feasible	Accessible and adequate sample size; sufficient expertise to address it; sufficient time and resources; manageable in scope
Interesting	The question that the researcher is sincerely interested and/or invested in
Novel	Builds on previous research but also offers something new
Ethical	Takes ethical issues into consideration; can be approved by the institutional review board
Relevant	Grounded in a theoretical framework; can suggest directions for future research; addresses some real problem in the world directly or indirectly

CHAPTER 4

Developing the Conceptual/ Theoretical Framework

The words *theoretical framework* and *conceptual framework* are among the most perplexing for research students. A firm knowledge of these two words is critical since they are required to create high-quality and trustworthy manuscripts (McKercher, Law, Weber, Song, and Hsu 2007).

Unfortunately, most students and faculty members often misuse the two phrases in their studies, weakening their conclusions.

Without a sound theoretical or conceptual framework, readers have difficulty determining the academic status of such works and the rationale for established hypotheses and research questions.

Thus, this chapter aims to improve researchers' comprehension of theoretical frameworks or conceptual frameworks.

The following components of theoretical and conceptual frameworks will be discussed in this chapter:

- Importance of theoretical framework and conceptual framework in research
- Selection of an appropriate theoretical framework

- Construction of an appropriate conceptual framework
- Steps to follow when developing the conceptual framework
- Checklist for the assessment of an effective conceptual and theoretical framework

Differences between Theoretical Framework and Conceptual Framework

Numerous studies use a variety of terminology to explain the two terms, yet all definitions have a fundamental basis.

The theoretical framework has been characterized as a road map or blueprint that directs the researcher throughout the study process (Fulton and Krainovich-Miller 2010). Additionally, the phrase refers to a collection of theoretical ideas, constructions, concepts, and tenets of a theory that guide the research process (Adom et al. 2016; Grant and Osanloo 2014).

On the other hand, the conceptual framework is described as the structure that explains the course of the event under investigation (Adom et al. 2016). Additionally, the phrase refers to how the researchers envision the link between the variables under investigation. Thus, the conceptual framework is described as the logical representation of the link between the study's primary ideas (Grant and Osanloo 2014).

The theoretical and conceptual frameworks might be presented graphically or narratively (Adom et al. 2016).

Unlike the theoretical framework, the conceptual framework focuses on specific or narrower ideas that are specific to the research question and the purpose and significance of the study.

The theoretical framework, on the other hand, positions the study within a broader worldview.

The theories that make up the theoretical framework are not the creation of the authors but concepts that have been tested and validated by other scholars. However, the researcher creates the conceptual framework using specific variables that are selected from the study's research questions.

The theoretical framework also differs from the conceptual framework in that the latter focuses on testing theories while the former aims at developing theories regarding the phenomenon of interest (Adom et al. 2016).

What Is the Importance of Theoretical and Conceptual Framework in Research?

Table 7 provides a summary of the importance of the theoretical framework and conceptual framework. The described benefits show that theoretical and conceptual frameworks are important components of research.

Therefore, students who aim to produce a quality publishable research paper need to consider incorporating theoretical and/or conceptual frameworks in their research.

Table 7

Importance of Theoretical Framework and Conceptual Framework in Research

Theoretical Framework	Conceptual Framework
The theoretical framework provides the researcher's philosophical, epistemological, and methodological definition of the study (Grant and Osanloo 2014).	The conceptual framework provides a platform upon which the researcher can develop his/her worldview on the phenomenon of interest (Adom et al. 2016).
It contextualizes the study within the existing literature and therefore positions it in a scholarly and academic fashion (Adom et al. 2016).	It provides the reasons the research is worth carrying out (Akintoye 2015).

It is the focus of the research, and its links to the research question guide the selection of the research design and data analysis approach.	It describes the researcher's assumptions regarding the relationship between the various aspects of the research phenomenon (Evans 2007).
It determines the type of data to be collected, and it allows for effective generalization of the study findings.	It provides the conceptual grounding of the research approach (Adom et al. 2016).
It opens up the researcher's worldview of the phenomenon of interest and provides a basis upon which the researchers can challenge their perspective against the competing theories (Akintoye 2015).	It is used as an alternative when the existing theories are insufficient to provide the logical research structure (Akintoye 2015).

Selection of an Appropriate Theoretical Framework

According to Grant and Osanloo (2014), no research has a flawless hypothesis. Therefore, how can one choose a single hypothesis and disregard the others?

The researcher's selection of an appropriate theoretical framework is contingent upon their thorough grasp of the study issue, goal, and importance, as well as the research question (Adom et al. 016; Simon and Goes 2011).

A proper theoretical framework also stresses the research's goal and significance (Grant and Osanloo 2014). Thus, while selecting a theoretical framework, researchers must ensure that the chosen theories are compatible with the research question and study objective (LoBiondo-Wood and Haber 2014).

Thus, the discussion of the research findings must gravitate toward confirmation, expansion, modification, or critique of the selected theoretical framework (Adom et al. 2016).

The questions that the researchers should ask themselves when selecting the theoretical framework include the following:

- Is there congruency between the selected theory and the methodology plan for the study?
- Are the theoretical constructs within the selected theory sufficient to guide the study?
- Is there congruency between the selected theory's concepts and the objectives of the study?
- Is there congruency between the selected theory and the problem, purpose, and importance of the study?
- Is the selected theory relevant to the discipline?
- Is there agreement between the selected theory and the research questions?
- Does the selected theoretical framework give relevance to the literature review?
- Is there agreement between the selected theory and the data analysis plan?
- Does the selected theoretical framework inform the discussion, conclusion, and recommendations of the study?

Construction of an Appropriate Conceptual Framework

It is the responsibility of the researchers to construct the conceptual framework (Adom et al. 2016; Polit and Tatano 2004).

The conceptual framework is built with diagrams that define the variables and show how they relate to one another. Although researchers can use existing frameworks, they must modify them to fit the specific research and research question. The developed conceptual framework also needs to agree with the research context (Latham 2017). Then after developing the graphical representation of the relationship between the different variables, researchers need to describe the diagram in the text (Fisher 2007). The following are examples of conceptual frameworks adapted from published articles. From the examples, it is evident that the conceptual framework needs to agree with the study title, and the objective and all hypotheses emerge from the conceptual framework.

Example 1 (Saleem 2015):

Title: The Impact of Leadership Styles on Job Satisfaction and the Mediating Role of Perceived Organizational Politics

Objectives: To investigate the impact of leadership styles on job satisfaction and to see if perceived organizational politics has a mediating role or not.

<<image here>>

Figure 1. The conceptual framework developed by Saleem (2015)

Study hypotheses:

H1: There is a relationship between transformational leadership and job satisfaction.

H2: There is a relationship between transactional leadership and job satisfaction.

H3: There is a relationship between transformational leadership and perceived organizational politics.

H4: There is a relationship between transactional leadership and perceived organizational politics.

H5: There is a relationship between perceived organizational politics and job satisfaction.

H6: Perceived organizational politics is a mediator between transformational leadership and job satisfaction.

H7: Perceived organizational politics is a mediator between transactional leadership and job satisfaction.

Example 2 (Rezvani et al. 2016):

> **Title:** Manager emotional intelligence and project success: The mediating role of job satisfaction and trust
>
> **Objectives:** To understand how project managers' emotional intelligence (EI) contributes to project success and to explore potential mechanisms by which an emotionally intelligent project manager may contribute to project success factors

<<image here>>

Figure 2. The conceptual framework developed by Rezvani et al. (2016)

Study hypotheses:

> H1: Project managers' EI is positively related to project success.
>
> H2: Project managers' EI is positively related to (*a*) their job satisfaction and (*b*) their trust in others.
>
> H3: There is a positive relationship between project managers' trust in others and project success.
>
> H4: Project managers' job satisfaction is positively related to project success.
>
> H5: Project managers' attitudes, namely (*a*) job satisfaction and (*b*) trust, mediate the relationship between project managers' EI and project success.

Steps to Follow when Developing the Conceptual Framework

The following steps need to be followed when constructing a conceptual framework:

1. Examine and understand the research title and research problem.
2. Determine the key variables in your research.
3. Review related literature to learn how to build assumptions regarding identified variables.
4. List the constructs and variables.
5. Document the assumptions regarding the relationship between the constructs and variables using graphical representation.

Checklist for the Assessment of an Effective Conceptual and Theoretical Framework

Table 8 provides a checklist for evaluating the conceptual and theoretical framework.

Table 8

Checklist for Evaluating the Conceptual Framework and the Theoretical Framework

Theoretical Framework	Conceptual Framework
Does it provide the philosophical, epistemological, and methodological definition of the study?	Does it provide the graphical representation of the relationship between the different aspects of the research phenomenon and research question?
Does it contextualize the study within the existing literature?	Is it grounded in the relevant literature?
Does it connect the research question to the research design and data analysis?	Does it describe the researcher's assumptions regarding the relationship between variables?
Does it identify the type of data to be collected?	Does it provide details regarding the research approach?

CHAPTER 5

Guidelines for Carrying Out a Focused Literature Review

A literature review is a multistage process that includes scanning for material, recording it, synthesizing and organizing it, and producing critical analysis of the evidence gathered. The literature review establishes the context for the whole study topic and is essential in determining what has been published about the subject before. Additionally, it places the identified research focus within the context of the relevant broader academic community, and a well-written literature review aids in the comprehension of the existing relationship between the various authors' contributions to the research area, identifies contradictions, and, if possible, suggests resolutions to these contradictions (McKercher et al. 2007). Notably the literature evaluation assists in identifying gaps or unresolved issues.

Students face various challenges when writing the literature review. These are some of the challenges faced when writing the literature review:

- Deciding on a topic for the literature search

- Identifying the relevant sources of information
- Extracting data from the selected studies
- Understanding how to link the information together and develop a critical analysis of the obtained information

Writing a focused literature review is central to an effective research process.

This section provides a stepwise approach to writing a literature review to ensure that the writing process is focused and associated with limited challenges.

Steps in Writing a Focused Literature Review

Creating a targeted literature review is a methodical procedure that involves many phases.

The stages outlined here are based on my own experiences, extensive study, and years of collaborating with seasoned authors.

While the processes are described sequentially, it is worth noting that some of the steps may be completed simultaneously.

The five steps for conducting an effective literature review are as follows:

1. Developing a mind map
2. Material search and extracting of relevant data
3. Piecing the ideas together
4. Developing a critical analysis

Developing a Mind Map

Before writing the literature review section, one needs to develop a mind map (Kalyanasundaram et al. 2017).

Mind mapping the literature can only be carried out once a research question has been developed (Hart 2018). Therefore, the first step in the development of the mind map involves the question *why*, which is answered by a clear and complete statement of your research question (Kalyanasundaram et al. 2017).

This is one example of a clear and complete research question: What is the impact of technological adoption on the cost of health care services (adapted from Okpala 2018)?

The second step is identifying the key terms, concepts, and phrases from the identified research question. This step involves the underlining of the terms that form the basis of the research question. The key terms (T1, T2, and T3) that can be identified from the example of research question provided above are shown in figure 3 below:

<<image here>>

Figure 3. Identification of the key terms within research questions for the development of the mind map

The third step involves identifying the questions that emanate from the terms that were placed in step two and the questions that flow from the research question as a whole (Kalyanasundaram et al. 2017).

During this step, it is also vital to develop generic questions that form the focus of the literature review (Hart 2018). Some of the generic questions include the motivations for research, such as the significance of the area of study, deficiencies in existing knowledge, sources of new ideas, and questions regarding the theory (Hart 2018).

Finally, the fourth step in developing the mind map is the development of follow-up questions and links to the questions in step three. An example of the mind map that is relevant to the example research question is provided in figure 4.

<<image here>>

Figure 4. An example of mind mapping

The development of the mind map is a continuous process that can stretch into the actual writing process (Kalyanasundaram et al. 2017).

Researchers should develop new questions and add to the map as they get new ideas from reading or engaging in discussion on various topics related to the research study (Hart 2018).

The mind map helps students address the challenges that were listed in the introduction, such as the identification of the relevant information and the topical areas that should be addressed by the literature review.

Material Search and Extracting Relevant Data

Relevant material includes that which was utilized in the composition of the literature. These sources may be accessed via electronic databases, information libraries, and the bibliographies of other resources.

- *Electronic Sources.* Searching electronic sources is probably the quickest way to access a lot of material. Electronic resources are material in digital format that is accessible electronically (Randolph 2009). Examples of electronic resources are electronic journals (e-journal), electronic books (e-book), online databases in varied digital formats, Adobe Acrobat documents (.pdf), web pages (.htm, .html, .asp etc.), and more.

  - *Identifying quality sources.* Web content is transient; it regularly changes, becomes obsolete, or gets erased.

    Due to the fact that most online content is not subjected to rigorous quality control, students are confronted with the issue of establishing the quality and relevancy of the information they gather (Randolph 2009).

The checklist in table 9 is recommended for evaluating the quality of electronic data.

Table 9

Checklist for Assessing the Quality of Electronic Sources

Item	Questions to Ask
Authority	Who is the author? Is there a way of verifying the legitimacy of the author? Is the writer qualified? Is the source known to be reliable?
Accuracy	Is it possible to verify the factual information? Can one opinion be verified against another? Is the material free of grammatical and spelling errors?
Objectivity	Is the material free of conflict of interest or bias? Does the material have any link to a company/organization or another web page? Is there any advertising? Is the statistical evidence credible? Is the language free from any partiality?
Currency	Is the chosen material up-to-date? Are the findings based on the most recent data? When was the material published? Are there more recent publications on the same topic?
Coverage	Is the topic of interest well-covered by the material with arguments that are well-supported? Is the material within the context of your research? Does the material add new information or update on the recent sources?

 ∾ *Identifying appropriate search terms/key words.* The research question is the primary source of the key words for your search (Cronin, Ryan, and Coughlan 2008). Unlike a topic, which gives broad key terms that may not be relevant to the study, the research question provides specific key terms (Randolph 2009).

The first step in identifying the key terms from the research question is choosing the words from within your question that are the most important to your search.

Figure 5 shows the key terms (T1, T2, T3, T4, and T5) that have been selected from the research question.

<<image here>>

Figure 5. Identification of key terms from research question

The second step is using the identified key terms to search the selected electronic database. Then from the obtained articles, identify alternative search words that are used and identify their synonyms. Use the identified alternative terms to carry out a further search in the selected electronic database.

- *Information libraries.* The brick-and-mortar library may house policy papers, standards, archival material, videos, and audio recordings that are not accessible online. Journal searches may also be conducted at the library, where the researcher peruses the most relevant articles for the chosen study subject (Cronin et al. 2008; Randolph 2009).
- *Material from the bibliographies.* After identifying the relevant research material and articles, additional arti-

cles can be obtained from the bibliographies of the relevant studies (Cronin et al. 2008).

- *Determining the quality of the retrieved articles.* After finding articles based on the research question, it is important to appraise the quality of those articles. The critical appraisal of the selected material aims at answering four main questions (table 10). The more no responses, the lower the quality of the article.

Table 10
Summary of the Critical Appraisal Tool

Question	YES	NO
Does this study address a clearly focused question?		
Did the study use valid methods to address this question?		
Are the valid results of this study important?		
Are these valid, important results applicable to my study population?		

Various useful tools exist that help in answering the four questions in table 10.

The available critical appraisal worksheets vary based on the nature of the selected article. The links to the various critical appraisal worksheets are provided in appendix I.

- *Extraction of Data.* Data are extracted from selected studies and other official documents. Thus, it is important for researchers to develop inclusion and exclusion criteria that are appropriate for their study. See Cochrane (2019) for further details on the development of appropriate selection criteria.

The data collection process is carried out using the data collection sheet. The data collection sheets vary based on the nature of the study (Randolph 2009). However, the data collection sheet should contain at least the following prompts:

- *Authorship/identity*—The name of the author, title of the study, date of publishing, and country of origin (where the data were collected)
- *Objectives and methodology*—Participants, recruitment procedure, data collection approach, data analysis, limitations, and strengths of the study
- *Results*—The relevant findings to the research question, baseline findings, completeness of the findings, and missing participants
- *Discussion*—Key conclusions, emerging gaps, and comparison with other studies

It is best practice for researchers to tailor the data collection sheets to fit their needs. It is also important for researchers to pilot their data collection tools to ensure effectiveness. The examples of the data collection sheets provided in table 11 indicate the variations that exist across different studies.

Table 11

Example of a Data Collection Sheet

Source	Data Collection Sheet Content
Brizay et al. (2015)	1. Article: Author, title 2. Year of publication 3. Publication type 4. Term used (PAR, AR, CBR, CBPR, or other) 5. Original definition of term 6. Cited definition of term, including source 7. Period of data collection 8. Country (where study took place) 9. Objective of article/study 10. Study type 11. Study methodology 12. Study target group 13. Who was the community partner 14. Community advisory board 15. Role of community partner 16. Who took initiative for the research 17. Results dissemination to community 18. Institutional Review Board (IRB) approval 19. Which institution gave IRB approval 20. Ethical approval by community 21. Which capacity-building activities took place 22. What was the added value of the community involvement 23. What were the negative aspects/limitations of community involvement 24. Did the community involvement lead to changes in the community 25. Funding agency 26. Other partners involved
Staggers and Blaz (2013)	1. Author, year of publication, country 2. Target group, number of participants 3. Method of CTG training 4. Other training components 5. Method of evaluation 6. Kirkpatrick level 7. Results

Piecing the Ideas Together

One of the mistakes students make when assembling information from numerous sources is discussing each source individually. While this is a straightforward procedure, the result precludes critical investigation of the numerous pieces of evidence and the identification of points of convergence and/or divergence (Hart 2018; Randolph 2009).

As a result, best practices dictate that researchers mention many sources in each paragraph. Three distinct strategies may be utilized to connect the gathered thoughts. Each technique is explored in detail below:

1. *Theme approach.* This is the most common way to organize literature reviews. Information from the different sources is extracted and categorized into themes. The different studies are then compared to how they address (i.e., support/contradict) the identified theme. The thematic approach is commonly used when explaining key themes or issues relevant to the topic (Cronin et al. 2008).

2. *Methodology approach.* The methodology approach is commonly used when discussing interdisciplinary approaches to a topic or when discussing a number of studies with a different approach.

3. *Chronological approach.* The chronological method is often employed for subjects that have been debated for an extended period and have evolved through time. The information is ordered chronologically, following how the subject has evolved through time. The important epochs of change are sufficiently recognized and delineated.

4. *Broad to specific guideline.* When organizing information using any of the three methods outlined above, it is pref-

erable, to begin with, to the big picture and work your way down to a single topic (figure 6).

It is critical to notice that the broad to particular strategy also applies inside the literature review's subsections and individual paragraphs. Each paragraph should begin with a subject phrase that conveys the overall and broad perspective (Randolph 2009).

The broad to particular strategy is appropriate for providing the context and related elements of the study issue that are not directly relevant to the topic but are necessary for connecting the many related, more extensive articles (Hart 2018).

When beginning with a more significant issue area, students should avoid making sweeping comments that are not specific to the study subject or the evidence given.

<<image here>>

Figure 6. Representation of the broad to specific guideline

The small triangles within the large triangle indicate the need to adopt the guideline within the subsections of the literature review.

Figure 7 below shows the broad to specific approach. In this example, the author is focusing on power dynamics in health care teams (submitted for publishing). He starts by providing the bigger picture through the discussion of the importance of effective health care in the provision of quality health care, which then allows him to introduce the importance of the balance of power.

The author then introduces the role of health care leaders in ensuring the balance of power in health care teams to achieve effective delivery of service, which leads to the gap that the study sought to address: developing a conclusive and in-depth under-standing of the strategies that managers can use to address power dynamics in health care teams (figure 7).

<<image here>>

Figure 7. The broad to specific approach in piecing together the information

Developing a Critical Analysis

The ability to critically assess the obtained information is based on the ability to recognize, analyze, and evaluate the reason-ing and forms of argumentation in the articles.

According to Klein (1996), critical analysis of the obtained literature is "giving reasons for one's beliefs and actions…recog-nizing reasons and conclusions, recognizing unstated assumptions, drawing conclusions, appraising evidence, and evaluating state-ments, judging whether conclusions are warranted" (2).

For one to carry out a critical analysis of the obtained infor-mation adequately, one needs to synthesize the work and succinctly pass judgment on the relative merits of the assessed research (Randolph 2009). One should also identify limitations within the research and identify the possibility of taking the research further.

The critical analysis of the assessed research exposes existing gaps, which is the main goal of the literature review.

Documenting the Different Steps of the Literature Review

For some research studies, such as the systematic review and meta-analysis, it is important to provide a detailed account of how the literature review was carried out.

One of the tools that can be used to document the literature review process is the PRISMA (Preferred Reporting Items for Systematic Reviews and Meta-Analyses) chart (appendix II).

The PRISMA chart identifies all the records identified from the database search and those identified from other sources.

The chart also describes the selection of the retrieved records by indicating the number of records that were eliminated at each stage of selection, along with the reasons for their elimination.

Finally, the chart provides the total number of studies that were fully reviewed.

Checklist for the Assessment of an Effective Literature Review

Table 12 provides a checklist for evaluating the literature review.

Table 12
Checklist for Evaluating the Literature Review

Item	Description
Introduction	Check if the area of interest, the purpose of the study and review, and methods used in retrieval of article are highlighted.
Organization	Check if there is proper use of headings.
	Check if there is a logical flow of ideas and good transition between sections.
	Check if there are proper citations.
Description of the used articles	Check if there is a story line that documents what was done, by whom, where and what was obtained, and the relevance to the study area.
Critical analysis	Check if each study is analyzed and critiqued.

	Check if there is analysis and critiquing across studies.
	Check if there is an identification of differences in argument and areas of convergence and gaps in knowledge.
Conclusion	Check if there is a summary.
	Check if the summary links to the research methods.

CHAPTER 6

Guidelines for Developing an Effective Research Design

The research design serves as a road map for carrying out research.

Study designs are research strategies and processes that range from broad assumptions to particular data gathering and analysis approaches (Creswell and Creswell 2017).

A research design is also chosen depending on the nature of the research topic or issue being addressed, the researchers' own experiences, and the study's intended audience. The researcher's traditions and views about the techniques of inquiry and the precise methods of data collection, analysis, and interpretation influence the study design (Cone and Foster 1993; Creswell and Creswell 2017).

The researchers' choice and type of study design influence the quality of their results in terms of validity, reliability, and generalizability.

Additionally, a suitable approach gives the information necessary for another qualified scientist to replicate the study and aids in establishing the legitimacy of the findings acquired (Baron 2008).

Researchers may struggle to effectively address the research question and complete the numerous research activities without a proper methodological design (Cone and Foster 1993; Kennedy-Clark 2013). Thus, this chapter outlines the many parts of research design in order to give suggestions for developing an effective research design that is aligned with the research topic.

This section discusses the following features of research methods:

- Organization of the methods sections
- The language used in describing the methods
- Selection of the appropriate research design
- Addressing the challenges in data collection
- Addressing the challenges in the selection of a data analysis approach
- The influence of your personal experiences in the selection of research approach
- Assessment of among the methodology is replicable, repeatable, and robust

Organizing the Methods Section

To make it easier to judge the trustworthiness of the provided conclusions based on the described methodology, researchers should ensure that the methods and findings sections have similar subheadings (Creswell and Creswell 2017).

Another tactic that may help readers follow the presented methods more efficiently is opening words or sentences in the methods section that connects to the objectives.

The Language Used in Describing the Methods

Passive and Active Voices

The methods section should be written passively or actively (Katz 2009).

The passive tense highlights the action and detracts from the activity's performer.

In addition, the passive tense establishes that the action takes precedence over the doer. However, since some research needs the reader to identify the action's performer quickly, the researcher should eschew passive voice in favor of active tense.

The active tense establishes a connection between the doer and the activity. "The researcher solicited volunteers through posters," for example, is written in the active tense. However, it should be emphasized that active voice sounds repetitious, which is why most researchers avoid it (Katz 2009).

The use of passive voice enables researchers to include historical data into their approach, which improves the flow (Creswell and Creswell 2017).

There are, however, problems that students need to look out for when using passive tense in the methodology. The major challenges that can render the methodology difficult to follow when written in passive tense are described below.

- *Very long subjects and a short passive verb right at the end.* This is an example of a confusing use of passive tense: "Two RCT studies and four intervention studies collected from Google Scholar, as well as one RCT article and three systematic review articles retrieved from PubMed, were used." This challenge can be addressed by placing both the subject and the verb in the first part of the sentence and the list of items at the end of the sentence: "Ten articles were used: Two RCT studies and four intervention studies collected from Google Scholar and one RCT article and three systematic review articles retrieved from PubMed."

- *Repetition.* The sentences should be abbreviated to avoid repetition.

Selection of the Appropriate Research Design

This chapter explores the design of the research by classifying it as quantitative or qualitative.

However, this does not imply that the author advocates for separatist thinking in selecting the study design (Kennedy-Clark 2013). Instead, the author recommends triangulation across several levels of the research to ensure data completeness and capture as much information about a given occurrence as feasible.

Furthermore, by emphasizing qualitative and quantitative alternatives, the author hopes to demonstrate the range of available options and how each may be employed to provide a holistic research approach.

The students should answer five main questions when choosing the appropriate research design:

1. What kind of data will I gather?
2. How will I gather the data?
3. From whom will I gather the data?
4. How will I analyze the data?
5. How will I present data?

When the student examines the research issue, they may see that it demands (*a*) a representative sample of several instances or (*b*) the variables to be evaluated in a controlled setting, which is characteristic of quantitative techniques.

Several quantitative procedures may be used, including surveys, experimental designs, and intervention strategies (Kennedy-Clark 2013). Alternatively, the student may observe that the question requires an in-depth examination of a few instances, which are the characteristics of qualitative techniques. Case studies and ethnography are two qualitative approaches that may be used.

Table 13 presents responses to the preceding topics, emphasizing quantitative and qualitative research methods.

Table 13

Choosing the Appropriate Research Design

Question	Quantitative Research	Qualitative Research
What kind of data will you gather?	Scores, frequencies, rankings	Stories, perceptions, descriptions, narratives
How will you gather the data?	Test, questionnaire, observation schedule	Participant observations, open-ended interviews, document analysis
From whom you will gather the data?	Representative sample: random or stratified samples	Theoretical cases, purposive samples
How will you analyze the data?	Mean, mode, frequency, distribution, inferential statistics	Constant comparative analysis, grounded theory, discourse analysis
How will you present data?	Graphs, tables, diagrams	Participant quotations, observer field notes, concept maps

Challenges to Expect when Using a Qualitative Design

The difficulties listed here are primarily those researchers investigating sensitive subjects are likely to encounter. Evaluating such challenges is intended to equip researchers better to solve them. One of the difficulties that researchers may encounter is desensitization.

Occasionally, listening to terrible experiences from others might result in researchers being unaffected by them (Dickson-Swift, James, Kippen, and Liamputtong 2007).

A researcher's lack of sensitivity to ordinarily sensitive events might result in the researcher's being perceived as an alien, which can have far-reaching consequences for social connections.

Researchers should be mindful of the danger of perceiving unusual cases or events as curiously typical (e.g., rape and other abuse accounts). Desensitization might have a detrimental impact by isolating researchers from their emotions (Dickson-Swift et al. 2007).

Another point to consider for qualitative researchers is the risk of *building attachments*.

Researchers who conduct sensitive studies run the danger of forming an emotional connection with their subjects, which may cause them to think about them long after the research is complete. Such ideas may have a detrimental impact on researchers in various ways, mainly if they are unprepared to cope with such occurrences.

Additionally, qualitative researchers can experience a *sense of vulnerability*, particularly when they are charged with collecting data in people's homes.

It is critical to highlight that qualitative research may sometimes give you the impression that you are learning about yourself, which heightens your sense of vulnerability. While listening to others' pain, researchers are sometimes confronted with frightening ideas about their death and fragility.

Additionally, researchers should be aware that qualitative research may result in *sentiments of guilt*.

Qualitative researchers should be mindful of the danger of experiencing guilt for the research's consequences on the participants. It should be highlighted that some of the sensitive material shared by respondents may cause them to recollect and relive the events, which might have severe emotional consequences for the respondents. When researchers see participants' breakdowns during interviews, they are often led to believe that they are only utilizing the participants as a means to an end.

Researchers may also feel guilty for perceiving the participants' awful experiences as "wonderful material" that will assist them in answering their study questions.

Exhaustion is a similar issue that qualitative researchers should be mindful of. Interviewing for sensitive material may be emotionally and/or physically draining.

Finally, listening to complex stories may sometimes instill a *sense of duty* in researchers. For instance, when researchers interview vulnerable rape victims who cannot defend themselves, the tales might weigh hard on the researchers' consciences, and they may feel compelled to intervene to protect the respondents.

How to Address the Challenges in Qualitative Research

It is critical for researchers who use qualitative designs to do proper preparation. They must establish strategies for overcoming any obstacles while obtaining sensitive data through qualitative research.

To address participants' concerns about the difficulties they face, researchers should be prepared with pertinent contact information for potential professional assistance and support (Dickson-Swift et al. 2007).

Additionally, researchers should do a risk assessment for themselves and the study subjects. Furthermore, the researchers must build a support structure to aid in the debriefing process.

This support system might be comprised of networks of colleagues, trustworthy friends, and family members who can advise and assist researchers in overcoming obstacles.

Additionally, researchers should consider establishing a peer support network that brings together a diverse group of researchers (Dickson-Swift et al. 2007).

The peer support program offers a place for researchers to discuss their experiences and build a professional network of confidants. Students, in particular, should make full use of professional supervision to get debriefing, mentoring, and skill development services.

Additionally, researchers should be urged to use self-care measures to safeguard against physical and mental injury. Researchers may use self-care practices such as debriefing, counseling, and arranging rest breaks during the study.

Researchers should allow participants enough time between interviews to digest any stories gleaned during data collection that may be detrimental to their emotional well-being.

Additionally, researchers must acquire techniques for coping with feelings and emotional connections and terminating their study engagement (Dickson-Swift et al. 2007).

Addressing the Challenges in Sample Selection

What Kind of Data Do I Need?

The answer to this question lies with the adopted research tradition. If you embrace objectivity in your research, as is the case with the positivist tradition, which is common in quantitative research, you need to have a *representative sample*. Otherwise, a *nonprobability sample* is adequate for those who embrace subjectivity, as is the case with the interpretivist tradition, which is common in qualitative research.

How Do I Obtain a Representative Sample?

Researchers can obtain representative samples through probability sampling techniques, including random, systematic, and stratified sampling. Random samples can be obtained by using a table of random numbers or a computer-generated random sample.

A systematic random sample can be obtained by choosing the nth item from a listed set of items. Categorizing subjects and randomly selecting from the categories can also result in a stratified random sample.

How Do I Obtain a Nonprobability Sample?

Sampling can be carried out using the nonprobability approach, such as purposive, theoretical, convenient, snowball, and quota sampling.

Purposive samples are selected based on the researcher's judgment and the study's objective.

Theoretical samples are selected based on the study's theoretical framework.

A convenient sample is easy to access and provides helpful information.

To obtain a snowball sample, the researcher asks the first subject to recommend another subject, who then recommends the next, and so on (Creswell and Creswell 2017).

Finally, a quota sample is made up of quotas for each category the researcher wishes to represent.

Addressing the Challenges in Data Collection

Before suggesting the ways to address the challenges faced during data collection, it is important to first highlight the major challenges.

The challenges presented in this book (and summarized in table 14) are based on my experiences and the knowledge amassed from reading various articles and books.

Table 14

Summary of Challenges Faced in the Collection of Data

Nature of Challenges	List of Challenges
Researcher-related challenges	Uncooperative respondents
	Lack of experience, such as in carrying interviews
	Isolation from peers and other researchers
	Researcher fatigue
Participant-related challenges	Concerns over confidentiality
	Anxiety
	Handling distressed participants
	Literacy level of the participants
Challenges associated with data collection venue	Potential for disturbance
	The nearness of family members or significant others
Challenges associated with the adopted research design	Process of designing an interview guide
	Length of time need to observe the phenomenon of interest

- *Researcher-related challenges.* The challenge associated with uncooperative respondents can be addressed by ensuring that the informed consent is used during the recruitment process to select participants who fully understand the study and their role in it. The use of informed consent also ensures that only those participants who are willing to take part in the study are selected.

During the data collection process, the researcher can solve the issue of uncooperative respondents by allowing and encouraging the respondents to voice their concerns and to skip the questions they do not feel comfortable answering. The respondents should also be reminded of their freedom to quit the study at any time.

The challenge associated with the lack of experience, such as that needed to effectively carry out interviews, can be addressed by ensuring that researchers carry out an extensive literature review on the topic to understand what other researchers have done. Depending on the chosen research design, the researcher can benefit from the knowledge of the respondents regarding the topic of interest.

The researcher should allow the respondents to express their knowledge and understanding of the research phenomenon and lead the process of knowledge development.

The challenge associated with isolation from peers and other researchers is a common problem that can be addressed through proper time management. The researcher needs to plan his/her time to ensure that there is time for private and social activities, which helps the researcher break from the research work and reconnect with friends and family.

The challenge of researcher fatigue is also associated with the failure to adequately plan time or poor framing of the research question, which can lead to the need for extensive research within a limited period and with limited resources.

In qualitative research, research fatigue can be limited by reducing the number of interviews conducted in a day.

It is also advisable to take thirty- to sixty-minute breaks between interviews. Debriefing with a colleague or advisor after doing a set of interviews also helps address fatigue among researchers.

- *Participant-related challenges.* The researcher should develop the questions based on the literacy level of the participants.

  There is also a need to pretest the data collection instrument among the nontarget population to identify the respondents' questions and restructure or delete the questions accordingly.

  The challenge associated with the concerns over confidentiality can be addressed during the recruitment phase.

  The researcher needs to disclose to participants the methods that will be used in securing their confidential information. The researcher needs to ensure that the research participants read and understand the content of the informed consent on data protection, privacy, and confidentiality.

  To ensure that the study adheres to ethical guidelines and to avoid privacy concerns, the researcher should only recruit participants who express satisfaction with the measures taken in the study to protect their privacy and confidentiality.

The researcher should also allow participants who change their minds regarding their satisfaction with privacy and confidentiality measures to withdraw from the study.

Concerns over privacy and confidentiality can also be addressed by allowing the participants to complete the data collection using alias names or by enabling the participants to use close cross-street addresses to their homes instead of their exact addresses (Rimando et al. 2015).

Ensuring that they understand their role in the study, how the information they provide will be protected and used, and their privacy and freedom to withdraw from the study without facing any consequences can address anxiety among the participants.

It is also essential to listen to the participants' concerns and provide breaks from data collection for the participants to compose themselves and only continue with the data collection after determining the participants are ready and comfortable.

Other techniques that can be used to manage anxiety among participants during data collection include the incorporation of icebreakers before the interview, which helps put the participants at ease with the interviewer.

- *Challenges associated with data collection venue.* Conducting the data collection in a neutral location helps address the challenges associated with the data collection venue. The chosen venue should be convenient and safe for both the participant and the researcher. Further, the location should allow participants to freely express themselves and the researcher to collect quality data.

- *Challenges associated with the adopted research design.* Beginning with the framing of the research question, the researcher should ensure that the research design that will be adopted will not demand the use of data collection tools that are hard to develop. Whenever possible, the adopted research design should allow the use of existing tools whose reliability and validity have been established (Creswell and Creswell 2017).

  If this is not possible, the researcher should use triangulation to help address the potential challenges faced when developing a data collection tool from scratch. Triangulation calls for the researchers to immerse themselves in the existing relevant literature to identify ways to help direct the development of data collection tools. In addition, it is best practice for the researcher to test the data collection tools to ensure their fit and reliability for the study.

Other Challenges

What If I Am Dealing with Hard-to-Reach Data Sources?

Students sometimes choose a research question that requires them to sample and collect data from hard-to-reach participants, such as houseless people; the lesbian, gay, bisexual, and transgender communities; individuals with rare medical conditions; people who use illegal substances; and the least-prevalent group in a given population (e.g., aboriginal people).

The challenge that such researchers face as a result is the difficulty of accumulating ample enough samples using random population samples (Bonevski et al. 2014). Attempts to use probability sampling on such difficult-to-reach populations are inefficient in both time and money.

To address this challenge, researchers are advised to adopt alternative sampling approaches, such as the nonprobability options, which include snowballing, social networking or respondent-driven recruitment, venue-based time-location sampling, targeted sampling, capture-recapture, adaptive sampling, and over-sampling of low prevalence population subgroups (Bonevski et al. 2014).

However, the challenge with using these suggested sampling approaches is selection bias and gatekeeper bias, which can limit validity, especially in quantitative research.

However, researchers can use these approaches because they are less concerned with representativeness and generalizability (Bonevski et al. 2014).

Another option is to involve community organizations to help access the specific socially disadvantaged groups. The researcher then uses a convenience sampling approach to select the accessed participants (Hoppitt et al. 2012).

To reduce the cost associated with recruiting members of the hard-to-reach population, researchers are advised to collaborate with community organizations and religious groups. Other available options that can be adopted by the researcher include direct mail, community outreach, and recruitment through a health education council (Keyzer et al. 2005).

What If the Participants Have Low Literacy Levels and Language Use?

The collection of data can also be affected by the inability of the respondents to understand the language that has been used in a data collection tool such as a questionnaire.

Researchers can address this problem by simplifying the readability of the study materials by using simpler language (Bonevski et al. 2014).

Alternatively, researchers are encouraged to translate materials into other more common languages (Bonevski et al. 2014; McMillan et al. 2009). If the problem persists, researchers are encouraged to use bilingual research assistants (Anderson et al. 2009; Eakin et al. 2006).

Other approaches that can be used to address the inability of the respondents to understand the language used are to involve culturally trained and skilled field-workers (Flory and Emanuel 2004).

Researchers can also opt to use locals or peers to conduct fieldwork, which can also help to address mistrust (Hing, Breen, and Gordon 2010; Ryan, Kofman, and Aaron 2011).

Sometimes the use of third parties, such as the hiring of locals or the use of bilingual research assistants, can introduce other problems, such as confidentiality concerns and cost-effectiveness of the research.

To address such challenges, the researcher should change the approach used in asking a question by adopting approaches such as the use of photo voice, which allows the researcher to use pictures and photos to tell the story (Hergenrather, Rhodes, Cowan, Bardhoshi, and Pula 2009).

What If the Respondents Cannot Access the Data Collection Tool?

Sometimes the research question requires the researcher to collect data from a hard-to-reach population that may not have access to the data collection tool (e.g., inaccessibility to a landline or mobile phone for telephone interviews).

In such a scenario, the researchers can be hard-pressed to find an alternative because they do not want to lose the hard-to-find respondents. The researcher can solve such problems by incorporating other data collection forms, such as face-to-face door interviews or online surveys (Bonevski et al. 2014; Shebl et al. 2009).

However, researchers should be cautious when supplementing the existing data collection with another form of data collection (e.g., supplementing online questionnaires with face-to-face interviews) because there is a high risk of introducing very low kappa agreement scores due to the lack of equivalence in the responses obtained (Bonevski et al. 2014).

Addressing the Challenges in the Selection of a Data Analysis Approach

The answer to which data analysis approach to use depends on the research question and the chosen research design (see chapter 3 and the beginning of this chapter for further information on the association between the research question and research design).

Analysis of Quantitative Data

The data analysis approaches that can be adopted by quantitative researchers involve the conversion of data to numeric forms followed by statistical analysis.

First, the data needs to be prepared by editing, identifying missing data, coding, data entry, and data transformation.

Data editing involves the inspection of the data for completeness and consistency. The data can then be inspected for missing data using approaches such as simple descriptive statistics.

Standard practice is that questionnaires that are missing more than 10 percent of the total responses should be eliminated.

The coding of data involves the assigning of a numeric value (e.g., male = 1, female = 2) to the data to facilitate data analysis using data analysis software such as SPSS (Statistical Package for the Social Sciences). Data transformation involves the changing of the data into a new format, such as the changing of a ten-point Likert scale to a five-point scale.

Data Analysis Options for Quantitative Data

The number of variables determines the quantitative data analysis approach.

For a single variable, univariate statistical analysis can be adopted, the bivariate analysis is adopted for two variables, and the multivariate analysis is adopted for the research question with several variables. The univariate statistics are focused on describing the variable by explaining the distribution (frequency distribution), central tendency (mean, mode, and median), and dispersion (range, variance, and standard deviation). The bivariate and multivariate focus on explanation. Examples of bivariate analysis include linear regression analysis, correlation (relationship), distribution, t-test, a one-way Analysis of variance (ANOVA), and scatter plot. (The selection of the appropriate bivariate analysis is outside the scope of this book) Examples of multivariate analysis include the MANOVA (multiple analysis of variance), Analysis of covariance (ANCOVA), cluster analysis, hierarchical linear modeling, logistic regression, and logistic analysis.

Common Analytical Software Used in the Analysis of Quantitative Data

- *Microsoft Excel.* The benefits of Excel are that it is free of charge, includes everything in one program, and can be password secured. However, the software is limited by slow speeds when analyzing large files, has a limited number of rows and columns, and is vulnerable to viruses.
- *Microsoft Access.* Also, free and easy to access and use, Access is limited by a low level of interactivity and difficulties in dealing with large databases.

- *Statistical Package for the Social Sciences (SPSS).* The use of SPSS is common due to the advantages associated with the software, such as its broad coverage of formulas and statistical routines; the fact that it allows importing data files from other programs; and the fact that it is annually updated to increase sophistication. Its use, however, is limited by its high cost, limited license duration, and confusion among the different versions due to regular updates.

Data Analysis Options for Qualitative Data

Qualitative data analysis is based on interpretative philosophy. The deductive and the inductive approaches are the two approaches in qualitative data analysis.

The deductive approach is based on the use of the research questions to group the data, which is then followed by the location of the similarities and differences.

The deductive approach is commonly used when the time and resources are limited or when qualitative research is a smaller component of a larger quantitative study.

The inductive approach involves the use of the emergent framework to group the data and then look for relationships.

The inductive approach is used when qualitative research is a major design of the inquiry.

The analysis of the qualitative data occurs in five major steps.

The first is the *organization of data* through transcription, translation, cleaning, and labeling of data.

The second step is the *identification of a framework*, which means the identification of the coding plan. The framework is important in structuring, labeling, and defining data.

The third step is *sorting of the data into the framework*, which involves the coding of data, modification of the framework, and the accurate and appropriate entry of the data. The fourth step is the *use of the framework in descriptive analysis*, which involves the arrangement of the responses in categories and the identification of the recurrent themes.

The final step is the *second-order analysis*, in which the researcher identifies patterns in the data and the respondent clusters and develops the sequence of events. The data are then searched to answer the research questions, and finally, the hypothesis is developed and tested.

The final step only applies to explanatory qualitative analysis, which is guided by the research question. With the exploratory qualitative analysis, this is guided by the data. The data analysis stops at step 4.

Examples of commonly used analytical software in the analysis of qualitative data are ATLAS.ti 6.0, HyperRESEARCH, MAXQDA, the Ethnograph 5.08, QSRN6, QSR Nvivo, Weft QDA, and Open Code 3.4.

The Influence of Your Personal Experiences in the Selection of the Research Approach

Consider your training and experience in selecting the appropriate design. Someone with experience in technical or scientific writing and statistics is likely to choose a quantitative design.

Researchers who are uncomfortable with challenging accepted approaches among some faculty through qualitative and advocacy/participatory approaches also gravitate toward quantitative designs, which are the traditional mode of research due to their carefully worked out procedures and rules.

However, researchers who engage in personal interviews and enjoy writing in a literary way are likely not comfortable with the qualitative design.

Researchers who like being innovative and working more within researcher-designed frameworks tend to gravitate toward a qualitative design.

However, researchers who prefer the flexibility of qualitative inquiry and the structure of quantitative research tend to use mixed methods.

Assessment of Among the Methodology is Replicable, Repeatable, and Robust

- *Replicable.* Quantitative researchers mainly need replicable research. The indicators of replicable research include the inclusion of control experiments, repeated analyses, and repeated experiments. Sampling also enhances the replicability of a given piece of research.
- *Repeatable.* A repeatable methodology gives enough detail so other researchers can carry out the same research. Researchers are therefore advised to provide sufficient details about the instrument used, study participants and how they were recruited, the procedure used in the collection of data, and how the data were manipulated and analyzed.
- *Robust.* Robust research is one that has sufficient data points that facilitate the determination of data reliability. Researchers, therefore, need to ensure that the findings of the manuscript that is submitted for publishing are based on sufficient data. Researchers should also examine the presence of bias, especially bias that might have been nullified by the control experiments.

Checklist for the Assessment of an Effective Research Design

There are sets of best practices that a researcher needs to demonstrate adherence to for a manuscript to be accepted and published. Some of the best practice guidelines are related to ethical standards, the health and safety of all participants, and standard guideline that governs different types of research, such as Consolidated Standards of Reporting Trials (CONSORT) statement for reporting randomized trials.

The researcher needs to determine the best practices that are related to the adopted research design and the field of interest. Table 15 provides a summary of the key guidelines that guide the development of the research design.

Table 15

Checklist for the Evaluation of the Research Design

Item	Description
Is the problem statement provided?	Check if the problem statement is stated along with the background statistics.
Is the literature review provided?	Check if the research design is grounded within the existing literature.
	Check if the definition of terms, variables, data collection tools, and sampling approaches is evidence-based.
Is the hypothesis stated?	Check if the relationship between the variables is hypothesized.
Are the variables described?	Check if the DV and IV and the intervening variables (if any) are provided.
	Check if the variable is measurable.
	Check if the unit of analysis is provided.
Are the indicators provided?	Check if the indicators (objective, event-based, subjective, or proxy) are described.
Are the levels of measurement provided?	Check if the scale is described as being nominal, ordinal, or interval.

Is the sampling approached described?	Check if the type of sampling is identified.
	Check if the sampling approach is supported by literature.
	Check if the approach used to determine the sample size is described and supported by the existing literature.
	Check if the approach used in the recruitment of the respondents is identified and fully described.
Are the methods well-described?	Check if the methods are identified and the rationale for the choice is provided.
	Check if the approach used in disqualifying other candidate methods is provided.
Is the data collection approach well-described?	Check if the data collection method is identified and justified.
	Check if the data collection tool(s) is identified and that rationale is provided, along with the validity and reliability.
Is the data analysis described?	Check if the approach used in the presentation of findings is provided.
	Check if the DV and IV and the approaches used to analyze data relating to each research question are identified.
	Check if the test for the reliability and the validity of the developed data collection tool is provided.

CHAPTER 7

Effective Presentation of the Findings

The analysis of the obtained data can yield several findings. Researchers should sift through the numerous results and identify the results that answer the research questions. The presentation of findings in dissertations and theses varies slightly from the approach used in presenting findings in a manuscript.

Typically, the length of an article is restricted, which means the number of results that are generated from a typical research project cannot be accommodated in a single article (Fah and Aziz 2006).

Researchers need to be concise but still be able to articulate the results so that the target audience can understand them. The researchers should have the ability to select the findings worth presenting, and they should be able to package the information effectively.

This chapter provides guidelines on presenting the findings in the manuscript to enhance the possibility of a positive publication outcome. The aspects of the presentation of the findings that are addressed in this chapter include the following:

- General considerations for organizing the findings

- Use of text in the presentation of the findings
- Use of tables
- Use of graphs
- Presentation of statistics
- Checklist for the evaluation of presentation of the findings

General Considerations for Organizing the Findings

The presentation of the findings should be simple, should proceed from general to specific findings, should be geared toward answering the research questions, and should be described using the past tense.

Use of Text in the Presentation of the Findings

The text is used to describe the findings that are presented in the tables and figures. The text should highlight the data and provide the interpretation, which makes reading the findings less difficult.

However, researchers should avoid repeating the information contained in the tables and figures in the written text (Fah and Aziz 2006). Instead, they should only highlight the most important results in the text.

In addition, researchers should avoid using colorful words when describing the results and instead use the data to convey the information. Terms such as *remarkably, clearly evident, extremely,* and *obviously* need to be avoided (Fah and Aziz 2006). The examples below show how text should and should not describe the findings.

The Text Used for Interpretation

This example lacks the interpretation of findings: "The average BMI of twenty teens before the intervention was 28.1 kg/m2 and was 23.1 kg/m2 after the intervention." However, this example shows how to interpret the findings: "The average BMI of twenty teens decreased from 28.1 kg/m2 to 23.1 kg/m2 after the intervention."

Use of Unnecessary Words

This example contains the unnecessary words: "It is clearly evident that the average BMI of twenty teens reduced from 28.1 kg/m2 to 23.1 kg/m2 after the intervention." The preferred way to report the findings is this: "The average BMI of twenty teens decreased from 28.1 kg/m2 to 23.1 kg/m2 after the intervention."

Use of Tables

Researchers should use tables to present the numerical values that answer the research question. The use of tables allows the researcher to summarize large sets of data.

The data presented in the tables can also be easily compared. Features of well-prepared tables include the title, columns, rows, and footnotes.

The title should be brief and specific; it needs to provide a summary of the variables in the columns and rows (Grange 1998).

Similar data should be presented in the columns (Fah and Aziz 2006).

The footnotes should be used to enhance the clarity of the information presented in the table. The footnotes are usually listed at the bottom of the tables and can be identified using the abbreviations such as *, †, ‡, §, ‖, ¶, **, ††, or #. The abbreviations used should be standard throughout the section.

To enhance the clarity of the information presented in the body of the tables, the researcher needs to ensure that standardized units and number of decimals are used.

The researcher should also adopt a systematic approach for the presentation of dates and timing.

Further, the fewest number of zeros possible should be used. For example, instead of having lines that delineate every cell, three lines can be used: two at the top to show the column heading and one to demarcate table end.

A symbol such as an asterisk (*) can be used to enhance the neatness of the presentation when highlighting the significant values (Fah and Aziz 2006).

Use of Graphs

Graphs are best suited to show trends in the presented data. They are also used to avoid a lengthy description of the findings in the text by providing visual emphasis. They should incorporate a title, figure legend, and footnotes.

The features of the figures have the same characteristics as those of the tables (Fah and Aziz 2006). Categorical data can be presented using bar charts, but 3D charts and graphs should be avoided because they make the reading of the values in the Y-axis cumbersome. The presentation of the values that change over time is best done using the line graphs.

Researchers should, however, practice caution when using graphs because there is a likelihood of losing the precision of the values that exist in the tables (Grange 1998). Researchers need to focus on what they intend to communicate: if the intention is to show trends, graphs should be used; otherwise, the communication of precise values should be done using tables.

Presentation of Statistics

Most of the manuscripts that fail to be accepted by the journals fail because of errors in the presentation of the statistics.

Researchers need to ensure the reported statistics are not only comprehensible by the average reader but also sufficiently rigorous to withstand the critique of experts (Fah and Aziz 2006; Ransohoff and Lang 1997).

To facilitate proper reporting of statistics, researchers need to have a good understanding of the meaning of the statistics. Researchers with a poor understanding of statistics are encouraged to seek help from statisticians.

Some statistics are best presented in the text, such as the mean and standard deviation, median, and normality testing (Ransohoff and Lang 1997). However, more complicated statistical tests that involve the assessment of several variables are best displayed in tables followed with brief prose.

Researchers need to ensure that the P values are quoted and correctly interpreted. For values with insignificant statistical values, the researcher should avoid indicating $P > 0.05$ but instead specify the exact P values. Where possible, the researcher should present the 5 percent confidence intervals (95 percent CI) along with the P values (Fah and Aziz 2006).

Components of the Discussion of the Results

The discussion should be provided as a stand-alone chapter after the results chapter. The components of the discussion chapter are these:

- *Restatement of the purpose of the research.* The discussion should start with the restatement of what is being researched.

- *Consolidation of the findings and linking with previous research.* The next step is to summarize methods, findings, and claims with references to the relevant existing literature.
- *Recommendations.* The discussion should highlight how the obtained findings link with the wider world and future research. The researcher should identify the areas that need further research.
- *Implications.* The implications refer to how the findings relate to the wider world. The findings can be discussed based on how it influences the practice (practice implications) or it influences future research (research implication).
- *Concluding restatement.* The concluding statements should be made up of reiteration of the overall findings and claims.

Checklist for the Evaluation of the Presentation of the Findings

Table 16 describes the checklist that should be considered when developing the presentation of the findings section.

Table 16

Checklist for the Evaluation of the Findings Section

Item	Description
Do the findings address the research question?	Check if the various aspects of the research questions are adequately addressed.
Is the section well-organized?	Check if the broader findings are presented first, followed by the specific findings.
	Check if the headings of the results align with the objectives/research questions and the methods.
Is the text well-used?	Check if the text is used to interpret the findings.
	Check if there is any use of unnecessary words.
Are the tables well-presented?	Check if the data in the table columns refer to similar variables.
	Check if the required number of lines are used.
	Check if the title, footnote columns, and the rows are well-labeled.
Are the figures well-presented?	Check if the data are presented using the appropriate figures.
	Check if the title and footnotes are well-labeled.
Are the statistics well-presented?	Check if the P values are correctly reported.
	Check if the P values are correctly interpreted.
	Check if the statistics are comprehensible to the average reader.
	Check if the statistics are correct.

CHAPTER 8

Formulation of an Effective Abstract

Abstracts give a synopsis of the article; they are generally the second most essential section of the article, after the title, that the reader evaluates to decide the article's relevance to their research interests. As a result, developing a decent abstract is a critical task for every researcher.

This chapter includes advice for inexperienced researchers and students who are unsure how to create an abstract or what should be included in it.

The following abstract features are explored in this chapter:

1. Definition of a good abstract
2. Importance of a good abstract
3. The preferred structure of abstracts
4. Summary of steps to take in writing an effective abstract

What Is a Good Abstract?

Knowing a good abstract is important because it guides what needs to be included in the abstract. The following is a summary of a good/effective abstract:

- Made of a single or multiple standalone paragraphs that are coherent and concise
- Provides an accurate, complete, and concise description of the different parts of the research paper (e.g., background/introduction, purpose of the study, methodology, result, discussion, and conclusion), usually in the order in which they appear in the paper
- Made of well-connected ideas
- Does not introduce any idea that is not covered in the paper
- The first sentence of the abstract should be compelling and engaging to the reader (Huston and Choi 2017)

Why Is It Important to Have a Good Abstract?

Researchers must invest effort in developing a good abstract for various reasons.

First, most readers skim the abstract due to time restrictions and decide if it is worthwhile to read the full article. Second, readers who do not have access to the entire paper make their purchasing choice purely based on the abstract. Third, effective abstracts increase the article's visibility.

What Is the Preferred Structure of Abstracts?

The answer to this question lies with the instructions provided by the selected journal. It is best practice to consult the journal before writing the abstract. Some journals provide a list of questions or headings for authors to use when writing their abstracts.

For journals that do not provide explicit instruction on the structure of the abstract, the researcher should analyze articles that have been published in the journal to determine the generally accepted approach. Although abstracts are typically made up of 250 to 350 words, researchers should consult the selected journal's instructions and guidelines on the preferred number of words.

To develop writing competence, students should read various abstracts and analyze the structure and how the information is connected.

The flow of the information in the abstract is based on how well the researcher understands the content of the research paper. Although an abstract requires the researcher to include the various sections of the paper, researchers should spend more time on the unique contributions of the research and how the findings were obtained.

The example below shows an abstract that was published in the *International Journal of Healthcare Management* by the author of this book.

The first sentence of the abstract provides background information. The second sentence provides the purpose of the study, and the third sentence provides a summary of the research approach. The fourth, fifth, and sixth sentences summarize the major findings of the article. Finally, the last sentence provides the overall conclusion of the study.

The US health care sector is among leading globally in the incorporation of advanced technologies in its operations.

This study evaluated existing data to understand how technological advancement in the US health care sector has impacted the cost of health care services and patient satisfaction.

The study was based on a quantitative analysis of twenty-four existing studies selected from various electronic databases.

The results indicate a significant increase in the cost of health care service due to technology adoption and other factors.

Increase in cost due to technology adoption is evident in the area of diagnosis (63%, P = 0.002) and patient monitoring (51%, P = 0.021). A significantly higher percentage was found, of patients that believe the adoption of advanced technologies leads to improved quality in diagnostic procedures (67%, P = 0.042), monitoring (79%, P = 0.004), and data keeping (85%, P = 0.032). Strategies need to be developed to manage costs associated with technological adoption while ensuring the delivery of quality services (Okpala 2018).

Summary of Steps to Take in Writing an Effective Abstract

1. Do a thorough reading of the research paper to develop a summarized approach in your mind.
2. Based on the conceptualized summary, develop a rough abstract without looking back at your research paper. Ensure you have captured the different sections of the paper but avoid copying and pasting key sentences from your article.
3. Revise the initial draft to address the limitation in the structure and flow, remove unnecessary information, add important details that had been left out, reduce wordiness, and correct grammatical mistakes and sentence structure.
4. Carefully proofread your final draft.

PART 2

Basic Guidelines on Journal Selection: The Packaging of the Research Material to a Manuscript

CHAPTER 9

Guidelines on Journal Selection

The publication of finished research is a methodical procedure that requires teamwork among the editor, reviewers, and
author.

The requirements for different journals vary. Specific journals have stringent requirements and standards and lengthy review
periods, which might lengthen the paper's publishing process. As a
result, researchers must choose a journal that meets their requirements and available time.

This chapter guides students and inexperienced researchers
through publishing their studies. This chapter discusses the following characteristics of publishing:

- What a researcher should do to successfully publish the
  manuscript
- Selection of the journal
- What to consider when selecting the journal

What a Researcher Should Do to Successfully Publish the Manuscript

Novice researchers and students to optimize their publication outcomes can use various strategies. The strategies are listed below:

- Develop a critical and strong framework for manuscript writing by reviewing manuscripts for fellow researchers and journals.
- Carry out due diligence and understand the quality assurance criteria that referees and editors use to be able to plan the research well and produce quality writing.
- Select the journal earlier during the initial stages of research to package the paper to meet the journal's specifications and maximize the chances of acceptance.
- Pay keen attention to the referees' reports and address all the concerns raised by the editor and the referees. Demonstrate to the journal editor how you have improved the manuscript based on the journal referees' reports.
- Cultivate honesty, an eye for detail, and patience when writing the manuscript.

Selection of the Journal

As indicated, the ease of publishing and the time to publish vary across different journals. It should also be noted that the size of the audience, professional prestige, and rewards vary across the various journals. Therefore, researchers need to choose a journal that fits their requirements.

When Is the Appropriate Time to Choose the Journal?

At the beginning of the research is the best time to start identifying the appropriate journal for the research. Researchers should have identified the journal by the time of writing the introduction and discussion sections (Huston and Choi 2017; Testa 2009).

Should I Choose Only One Journal?

According to guidelines to publishing scientific research by Huston and Choi (2017), it is not advisable to select only one journal. Rather, Huston and Choi argue that one should select at least three and a maximum of five journals.

The chosen journals should be ordered in terms of journal impact factor. As will be discussed later in this chapter, the selection of three to five journals is important in the event of rejection of the manuscript by the first journal selection.

What to Consider when Selecting the Journal

- *Time taken to publish.* When selecting the appropriate journals for your manuscript, it is important to consider your preferred time of publication (i.e., how long you are willing to wait before the paper is published).

  The issue of time is particularly vital for researchers whose progress in their career or academic progress depends on the successful and timely publication of their manuscripts.

  However, it should be noted that the issue of time limitation when selecting a given journal can be addressed by planning, executing, and completing your research early enough to give sufficient time between publishing and your academic or career timelines (Guyatt and Haynes 2006). Thus, researchers should identify the journal early enough and be familiar with its publishing demands to plan the research and prepare in advance (Huston and Choi 2017).

Researchers need to check on the time taken by the journals to publish the received submissions. The average time to publication can be obtained from the journal's website.

- *Desired professional prestige.* Another consideration is the required level of professional status. Journals with a good reputation are often strict in their acceptance criteria and publish only articles that meet tight criteria. Researchers interested in publishing in such journals should ensure that their research strategy, subject selection, data presentation, writing quality, and explanation of results all comply with all applicable regulations (García et al. 2014).

- *Access to the desired audience.* Another factor that is important to consider is access to the desired audience (Huston and Choi 2017). The journal you choose should allow access to your target audience. For example, if your target audience is upcoming researchers in developing countries, it makes more sense to publish the article in open access journals because most of the target audience may lack access to paid/subscription journals. If the target is a large section of the population distributed across different academic and geographical divides, the researcher should avoid journals with limited distribution. New journals are likely to have a limited audience.

- *Is it peer-reviewed?* Another factor that needs to be considered is whether the candidate journals have peer reviewers (García et al. 2014). The peer-review process is essential for establishing the quality of your work and the development of your research profile. Thus, all researchers should consider publishing their work in peer-reviewed journals (Dougherty, Freda, Kearney, Baggs, and Broome 2011).

- *The scope and aims of the journal.* Every journal publishes its aims and scope on its website, and the scope and aims of the journal influence the readership.

  It is important to check the described scope and aims to determine whether they are aligned with the aims of your study (Huston and Choi 2017).

  The likelihood of your paper being accepted by the selected journal also depends on the articles that you have cited in the introduction and the discussion sections of your paper. Thus, researchers should read their introduction and discussion to develop a mind map of the frequently cited articles and related journals. Such information will aid in the selection of the journal that is likely to accept the work.

  However, as previously stated, the selection of the journal should occur before the writing of the introduction and discussion (García et al. 2014). This is important because it will ensure that the articles used in completing the sections are from the preferred journal.

- *Journal impact factor.* One of the factors that a researcher should consider when selecting a given journal is the quality of the journal and its contribution to research in the discipline of interest (García et al. 2014). It should be noted that there is no easy way of determining the quality of a given journal and differentiating between different journals.

One of the proposed approaches is to use the journal impact factor, which is based on the number of times an article that is published in a journal of interest is cited within a given period (García et al. 2014).

The journal impact factor for a given year is described as the mean number of times articles published in the journal in the two previous years have been cited in that year. The impact factor, therefore, simply gives the average recent use of the articles in the journal.

The other measure that researchers can use to judge the quality of the journal of interest is the journal immediacy index, which describes how rapidly the average articles are used in the journal.

The journal immediacy index is obtained by dividing the total number of articles that are cited in a year by the total number of articles that are published in that journal in that year.

- *Free or paid journals.* Some journals charge fees for publishing manuscripts. Thus, researchers need to be aware of the terms of publication to avoid unforeseen inconveniences.

For journals that charge fees for publishing manuscripts, researchers need to establish the criteria used to determine the total cost of publishing and plan appropriately (Dougherty et al. 2011).

CHAPTER 10

Packaging of a Quality Manuscript

After the completion of the research and all the sections of the paper (introduction, literature, methods, findings, discussion, and conclusion) have been written, the researcher should then repackage the information into a quality thesis based on the journal requirements. In the case of students, this involves the repackaging of the vast information contained in the thesis to fit the requirements of the selected journal.

Important factors to consider when developing the manuscript include clarity, relevance, and avoidance of plagiarism. This chapter discusses these features of quality manuscripts:

- Clarity of manuscripts
- Relevance of manuscripts
- Avoidance of plagiarism
- Assessing the quality of a manuscript

Clarity of Manuscripts

Novice researchers and students often fail to differentiate between thesis and manuscript writing and thus lack logical clarity. Conversely, manuscripts with a high level of clarity tend to have a higher chance of being published. This section provides a discussion of the strategies for achieving clarity in manuscripts.

Strategies for Achieving Clarity

- *Carefully plan every section of research.* Researchers who intend to publish their findings need to have foresight from the early stages of research planning, execution, and writing (Young 2002). Thus, researchers need to consider the various aspects of manuscript writing during the initial stages of study design.

  The creation and use of program resources, survey instruments, or other written products needs to consider the requirements that should be met for the paper to be published in the selected journal.

  This further demonstrates why it is important to select the journals during the early stages of project design. It is important to ensure that the materials that are used in research are easily understandable, grammatically and mechanically correct, and free from misspellings and inconsistencies.

- *Develop an outline and stick to it.* The use of an outline helps a writer organize thoughts before writing. The outline also enhances clarity by breaking down the topic, which can help identify potential weaknesses in the argument. In addition, the outline helps the writer identify the supporting details required to make the discussion of the significant aspects compelling and complete. Finally, the outline also ensures that researchers remain focused on the subject and avoid the back and forth in writing, confusing the readers.

- *Ensure coherence on both macro- and microlevels.* A coherent manuscript should flow like a story where the different parts contribute meaningfully to the whole. Therefore, researchers should ensure that although the different sections convey unique information and are stand-alone, they should be interlinked by consistent concepts and thought processes. In addition, the various sections and subsections of the manuscript need to be identified using clear and appropriate headings and subheadings.

  Finally, it is also important to avoid redundancy in writing (Young 2002). Researchers should avoid reformulating the same points across the different sections of the manuscript.

- To enhance coherence, the paragraphs should be kept as short as possible while ensuring that unnecessary breaking up of information is avoided. Repacking the content rather than breaking up the paragraphs can shorten long paragraphs. Each of the paragraphs should have a topic sentence that helps readers digest the dense and complicated content, while transitions link the subsequent paragraphs to the information within the paragraphs (Caelli, Ray, and Mill 2003).

  When numbering the sections and subsections within the manuscript, it is important to be consistent. Enhanced coherence can also be achieved through the use of a consistent language when referring to a specific item or phenomenon. Choose the definition to adopt a specific phenomenon and stick to it. Caution should be exercised when using synonyms because there is a high risk of repetition (Caelli et al. 2003).

Coherence is also achieved through the adoption of parallel construction of the different sections, such as the headings and the paragraphs. Further, parallelism in grammar should be adopted through the development of the sentences with the same grammatical structure. The content also needs to be organized logically. The ordering of the items needs to adopt a logical order either through alphabetical or chronological ordering (Caelli et al. 2003).

- *Proofreading.* Proofreading of the completed work is important in identifying and correcting grammatical and structural errors. The researcher should read the paper and correct any mistakes.

Additionally, it is advisable to have a colleague read your manuscript—preferably a colleague who is not familiar with your research. Having a different person read your work helps identify areas that might confuse the readers. Your colleague will also help judge the quality of your work and suggest areas that need to be improved (Young 2002).

Choice of Language

Language is a powerful tool for conveying information. Avoid offensive language and use accepted language when describing racial and ethnic identities of study participants. Do not use jargon and buzzwords. It is also best to avoid ambiguous or illogical comparisons (Messuri 2015).

To get a grasp of the preferred language, researchers should read journals and note the language used in the description of the research design, data analysis, and discussions.

Achieving Clarity through a Consistent Flow of Ideas

Consistency is one of the most important features of research writing and reporting.

Students need to ensure consistency in the content, structure, and language used in their research and manuscript. Ensuring consistency in research writing avoids sidetracking into areas that are not aligned with the topic (Pierson 2004).

Students and novice researchers also need to embrace consistency as a time-saving technique. (More time-saving approaches will be discussed later in this book.)

By adopting consistency in research, the researcher avoids problems such as collection of data that do not address the title and the study purpose and the back and forth in writing caused by the need to clarify inconsistencies (Pierson 2004).

Building Consistency between the Problem Statement, Title, Purpose, and Research Questions

The problem statement, title, purpose, and research questions form the first part of the manuscript that the readers encounter.

Establishing consistency in the problem statement, title, purpose, and research questions makes the logical arrangement of the other sections of the manuscript attainable (Oliver 2011).

To achieve consistency in the problem statement, title, purpose, and research questions, researchers need to ensure they identify the concepts or constructs of interest. The identified concepts of interest, then make the basis upon which the literature is used to develop the problem statement and purpose.

The identification of the concepts, as indicated earlier in this book, is based on the developed research question. Although the title may be continuously updated throughout the writing process, it is important in the early stages of the research because it provides the key words and relationships that guide the formulation of the problem, purpose, and research questions (Pierson 2004). Therefore, one feature of a good title is its consistency with the other parts of the research.

To ensure consistency between the title and the problem statement and the purpose of the research, there is a need to ensure the *why* and *what* aspects of the sections are fine-tuned.

The *why* of the title provides the need and importance of the research. Thus, it is important to ensure that the title justifies the importance of the study.

Providing a justification of the study in the title can ensure this and verify the problem statement and purpose of the research builds on that justification (Neale and West 2015).

Relevance of the Manuscript

The relevance of the manuscript is a rarely discussed topics in the preparation of the manuscript, yet it is one of the most important considerations by the editor when deciding on whether the manuscript should be sent to the referees. It is the responsibility of the editor to ensure that the manuscripts that are accepted are relevant to the audience that the journal serves.

It is also the responsibility of the researcher to ensure that he/she chooses a journal whose aims and scope agrees with the study objectives and the research questions (Ali 2010).

This section provides an in-depth description of manuscript relevance and what the researchers should focus on to ensure that the manuscript is relevant.

What Determines Relevance?

Understanding what determines the relevance of the manuscript is important in designing and the writing of the manuscript. In scientific research and journals, the mission of the journal, its scope, and the work of its readership determine the manuscript's relevance.

What Are the Conditions for Relevance?

- *The relevance of the content and the research question.* The editor and the reviewers judge the relevance of the manuscript based on its propriety for the journal, which indicates the suitability of the manuscript to the readership's interest and the focus of the journal. The propriety of the manuscript for the journal is based on the determination of the extent to which the topic of the manuscript and its research questions overlap or touch the scope of the journal (Dougherty et al. 2011).

  For example, say the editors ask, "Does the topic of the manuscript address some sections of interest to the journal focus?" Irrespective of the quality of writing and impact of the findings, the editors, with the help of the reviewers, can still reject the manuscript out of hand if its topic does not overlap with the focus of the journal.

  It is therefore important for researchers to thoroughly examine the foci of the journals of interest to determine whether they overlap with the aim of the study (Dougherty et al. 2011).

  The researchers should determine the importance of the manuscript to the journal through the judgment of the magnitude of the overlap that exists between the manuscript topic and focus of the journal.

The manuscripts that are regarded as being important (based on their propriety to the focus of the journal) are subjected to further scrutiny to determine their relevance within the journal's field of interest.

The editors use various aspects of the manuscript topic and subject in judging its importance. One consideration is whether the manuscript addresses what is considered a serious problem. The manuscripts that focus on real problems that are within the journal's area of interest are considered to be relevant. Such manuscripts should be able to provide practical solutions to the identified problem (Ali 2010).

Apart from establishing the fact that the research problem is serious, the editors also assess whether the problem is common. The editors will consider manuscripts that focus on problems that are prevalent enough to affect a large proportion of the population (Dougherty et al. 2011).

The interest in the articles that focus on common problems is based on the idea that more readers will tend to focus on common problems so the journal will attract more readers.

Editors also give priority to manuscripts that address the root causes of the problem. The researchers should, therefore, ensure, during the design stage, that the study is geared toward addressing the mystery of the mechanism of how the problem has evolved.

Lastly, the editors are also concerned about whether the study addresses a problem that has broader societal implications.

- *The rigor of the research approach.* The relevance of the manuscript and its suitability is also based on the research methods. For example, if the editors and reviewers ask whether the methods used are credible and sufficient enough to make the readers to adopt the research results with confidence and to apply them in another setting, the editors are concerned with both the adequacy of the research methodology in the research setting and its adequacy when applied to other settings.

The aspects of the research methodology that the editors look for include whether the adopted methods result in findings that are generalizable to different settings and whether the adopted methodology has any influence on the work of future researchers and policymakers (Katz 2009).

Determination of Relevance for Different Kinds of Studies

The relevance of the different studies varies based on the aim of such studies. For example, the relevance of studies that focus on cause and effect is based on the power of the causality. Thus, researchers who carry out cause-and-effect studies need to ensure that their studies demonstrate at least strong effects of innovation or otherwise show power to establish causality of the innovation (Katz 2009).

For studies that deal with assessing processes, the determination of the relevance is based on the quality or value of the process or procedure itself. Therefore, researchers whose topics deal with

111

the examination of a process need to ensure their findings provide an elaborate description of the performance of the examined process or the quality of the products obtained from the examined process. Thus, it is recommended that researchers need to understand and demonstrate how their research influences the readers or at least adds value to their work or way of thinking.

Originality and Topicality

Researchers need to ensure the manuscript meets the originality and topicality requirements.

The originality and topicality of the manuscript are established by situating the arguments on authoritative research (Katz 2009).

Originality and topicality can also be demonstrated by referencing recent literature. For example, the researchers who situate their research question on the foundation that the problem of interest warrants investigation because it has not been investigated for several years need to anchor such arguments on recent research that shows new developments in data gathering techniques or evidence from indirectly related fields that demonstrate research into the problem is required (Dougherty et al. 2011). However, researchers should not fall into the trap of looking for recent literature at the expense of not using seminal research that may be important in anchoring the methodology and the theoretical framework.

Manuscript Relevance Checklist

Table 18 provides a summary of the major aspects of the manuscript that determine its relevance to the selected journal. Students need to ensure that their manuscript fulfills each of these aspects.

The checklist provided in table 18 may not be exhaustive because the different editors and journal may have varying relevance determination criteria; therefore, researchers should thoroughly assess the relevance criteria that are unique to the selected journal.

Table 17

The Summary of the Major Aspects of the Manuscript that Determine Its Relevance

Item	Description
Item 1	Is the research relevant to the focus of the journal or its audience?
	Does the manuscript address vital problems?
	Is the study worth doing?
	Do the quantitative studies have accepted a level of generalizability? Is the participant selection process transparent, and are the setting and intervention or materials well-described?
	Do the qualitative studies offer theories that are generalizable or transferable to other contexts and people?

Avoiding Plagiarism

Plagiarism is the act of presenting other researchers' work without fully acknowledging them.

In research, the work is considered plagiarized if it contains ideas, methods, or writings from others that have not been fully acknowledged (Wajdi, Sumartana, and Hudiananingsih 2018). Plagiarism is therefore a form of copying or stealing other people's ideas. It should be noted that most plagiarism in academic writing and research is committed unintentionally or through reckless writing (Roig 2006).

Therefore, researchers need to understand the different forms of plagiarism to avoid committing such offenses.

Avoiding plagiarism should form the basis of writing quality manuscripts. Committing plagiarism in research constitutes a dishonest act and is therefore considered a breach of ethical principles, which can lead to the rejection of the manuscript (Roig 2006). Plagiarized work can also have long-term effects on the researcher's career and should be avoided at all cost.

Forms of Plagiarism to Look Out For

- *Verbatim quotation without clear acknowledgment.* This is where the author quotes the work of another researcher word for word without acknowledging them. Such quotations should be identified by the use of either quotation marks or indentation and with full referencing of the sources (Kumar, Priya, Musalaiah, and Nagasree 2014). Citing the quotation varies based on the writing format. An example in APA format is like this: "Insert the text" (author, year of publication, page number).

- *Cut and paste from Internet sources.* Material that is obtained from Internet sources needs to be acknowledged fully by indicating the author or the organization.

- *Paraphrasing.* Paraphrasing is the most common form of plagiarism that is committed by students. This form of plagiarism is committed due to poor writing style or time pressure, or students do it intentionally.

  Paraphrasing can result in plagiarism if the writer adopts the same reporting structure or makes a limited alteration in a few words and the order of arguments without acknowledging the source (Roig 2006).

However, students need to note that acknowledging the sources of the paraphrased worked does not fully serve to exempt the writing from being classified as plagiarized. Thus, you should attempt to write a summary of the author's overall argument in your own words.

- *Inaccurate citations.* This is a form of plagiarism that is often committed unintentionally by students, especially when using and acknowledging information obtained from a secondary source, not the primary source.

Sometimes students write the entire article, then go on a fishing expedition to look for articles to support their work, and they end up including articles and books in their references or bibliography they did not consult.

Another form of plagiarism is auto-plagiarism, where an author fails to acknowledge the use of his or her previous work; another is the failure to acknowledge assistance that was received during the completion of the work such as the acknowledgment of the contribution of statisticians (Roig 2006).

What Are the Consequences of Plagiarism?

In research, plagiarism has far-reaching consequences. Plagiarized articles can result in the withdrawal or the retraction of the article, cancellation of the article, and the replacement of the article (Wajdi et al. 2018). Authors who commit plagiarism may also face the additional punishment of being banned from sending articles to the affected journal.

Should Every Sentence Be Cited?

Not all sentences need to be cited. Some of the content in your article may constitute general common knowledge, which needs not be cited.

General common knowledge varies across different fields, and the author with good mastery of the field should be able to distinguish general common knowledge from what is not (Kumar et al. 2014).

Information that is considered to be in the public domain, such as the generally accepted dates of historical events such as World War I and II, is considered general common knowledge and therefore needs not be cited.

Additionally, field-specific common knowledge also does not need to be cited. An example of field-specific common knowledge is the fact that salivary amylase that is produced in the mouth helps in the digestion of starch. However, the author needs to ensure that the field-specific common knowledge used and not cited is widely known within that field and understood as such by the target audience (Roig 2006).

When to Paraphrase and When to Quote

The frequency of quoting or paraphrasing varies across different fields. For humanities papers, quoting is common while summarizing is common in social or natural sciences. The use of quotes is often aimed at showing that an authority supports the point that you are putting across. Quotes are also used when one is trying to present a position or argument to critique (Kumar et al. 2014). The use of quotes in research papers also helps preserve the meaning of passages that can otherwise be lost if they are paraphrased or summarized. However, if the language used is not of much importance as the idea, authors are always encouraged to summarize the work of others and put the writing in their own words.

How Can I Avoid Plagiarism?

Students and novice researchers can avoid plagiarism through diligent writing. Various recommendations, such as those listed below, can be taken to minimize the occurrence of plagiarism in written articles (Kumar et al. 2014).

- *Understand the context.* It is important to understand the ideas well enough to be able to restate them in your own words. Read and understand the passage as a whole.

- *Be selective.* You need to identify what needs to be para-phrased or quoted. Only use the sections of written work that will help you make a point.

- *Read while taking notes.* To ensure your article consists of your own words, spend time reading other researchers' work while writing down the main points to incorporate into your work. The written notes can then be used to develop arguments using your own words but acknowl-edging the source of the incorporated notes.

- *Changing the words and structure.* Some texts can be hard to summarize without altering the meaning. In such scenarios, if the author does not want to quote the text, it is advisable to change the structure by starting at a different place in the passage. The author can also break up long sentences and combine short ones. The second step is to change the wording by using synonyms or a phrase that expresses the same meaning.

- *Manage your citations.* It is important to maintain a record of sources while writing rather than searching for relevant source articles after completing the writing. The commonly used examples of software that help in the management of citations are EndNote and Reference Manager. Avoid referencing the literature review of a given article as the primary source of information, but instead reference the individual articles referred to in the review.

What Tools Can I Use to Check Plagiarism?

Commonly used tools to check plagiarism include Turnitin, Similarity Check, iThenticate software, PlagScan, and Plagiarism Checker.

Assessing the Quality of the Manuscript before Submission

Table 18 provides a summary of the points that should be considered when assessing the quality and readiness of the manuscript for submission.

Table 18

Checklist for Assessing the Quality of the Manuscript

Section of Interest	Criteria
Title	Check if the title accurately reflects the paper content.
	Check if the significant words in the title are near the beginning.

Abstract	Check if the abstract adheres to the required number of words.
	Check if the abstract summarizes all the required paper sections, including the introduction, purpose, methods, results, discussion, and conclusion.
	Check if the selected key words best allow the locating of the study.
Introduction	Check if the introduction begins with a broad issue related to the research area and narrows to the specific gap.
	Check if the relevant literature that is related to the research topic and that leads to the research gap is described in the introduction.
	Check if the introduction identifies the statement of the problem and the aim/hypothesis of the research.
	Check if it describes the originality of the research objectives by establishing the need for investigations in the topic area.
	Check if it gives a clear idea of the target readership.
	Check if it gives the originality and topicality of the manuscript.
	Check if the originality and topicality has been met by examining how the literature is used to anchor the research questions.
	Check if the information presented in the introduction naturally leads to the aim. You need to review the introduction if the explicit aims come as a surprise.

Methods	Check if the methods including statistical analysis appropriate for the questions addressed and the study.
	Check if there is clear and elaborate description of materials and methods in a manner that allows the determination of the credibility of the results.
	Check if the research is replicable.
	Check if the research is repeatable.
	Check if the research is robust.
	Check if the research has adhered to best practice.
Results	Check if the results provide answers to the questions raised in the introduction or address the study objectives.
	Check if the results are presented in a logical order in which the aims and the methodology are presented.
	Check if the tables and figures used in the manuscript are relevant and actually required. Could any be combined or deleted? Do they stand alone?
	Check if there is coherence in the description of results.
	Check if the findings are presented in the simplest possible terms.
	Check if the presentation of the findings makes reference to statistical analyses, such as significance or goodness of fit.
	Check if the results are plausible.
	Check if the observed trends support the paper's discussion and conclusions.

Discussion	Check if the original aim/hypothesis/question are mentioned in the beginning of the discussion.
	Check if the discussion has provided adequate comparison of the results and the relevant findings from the literature.
	Check if the discussion has provided adequate reasons or speculation regarding the observed similarities and differences between the results and the relevant findings from the literature.
	Check if the discussion provides adequate statements regarding the significance of the findings, inherent limitations, and implications for practice and/or future research directions.
	Check if the discussion evaluates the trends observed and explains the significance of the results to a wider understanding.
	Check if the discussion gathers all information into a single whole.
Conclusion	Check if the appropriate conclusion is based on the findings and discussion is provided.
	Check if the conclusion reflects upon the aims, and determine if they were achieved or not.
	Check if the conclusion is evidence-based.
References	Check if the references are complete and based on the required format.
	Check if the references adequately support the important parts of the argument.
	Check if the references are relevant.
	Check if the references are recent.
	Check if the references are readily retrievable.

CHAPTER 11

Interaction with the Editors

Authors and editors constantly communicate during the period between the submission of the manuscript and the final decision on whether to publish it or reject it.

For researchers who are new to article publishing, communication with the editors can be daunting, especially when the submitted manuscript is heavily criticized.

This chapter provides guidelines on how researchers should communicate with the editor. The aspects that are addressed include the following:

- Responding to editors
- How to address the rejection of a manuscript

Responding to Editors

Given the time that the researcher has to spend writing the manuscript, it is sometimes challenging for them to accept critical comments about their work. However, for the successful publication of the manuscript, the researcher should be open to the fact that he or she is rarely completely right or completely wrong (Cummings and Rivara 2002).

Similarly, the researcher should be aware that the referee or editor is rarely always completely correct or completely incorrect. Therefore, when addressing the referee's or editor's comments, the researcher should strive to address the comments without compromising the message of the paper (Guyatt and Haynes 2006).

When addressing the editor's comments, it should not appear as though you are trying to demonstrate that you know it all. Rather, you should demonstrate a willingness to learn and improve the paper (Cummings and Rivara 2002). If the manuscript is rejected, you should consider other journals.

How to Address the Rejection of a Manuscript

It is disheartening when a manuscript is rejected, and it can cause anxiety and panic when you are under pressure to submit and publish within a limited period. Thus, it is important to adequately prepare, do quality writing, and choose the appropriate journal to avoid rejection (Day 2011). However, despite one's best efforts, a manuscript can be rejected for one reason or another.

The rejection of the manuscript does not necessarily mean that the presented science is wrong. In fact, rejection is common.

A short talk with established researchers will demonstrate that most of them have had their manuscripts rejected at some point in their careers (Peregrin 2007). Discussion with someone in your discipline about rejection helps calm the nerves and allows one to focus on getting the work published (Peregrin 2007).

The first step a researcher should take following the rejection of a manuscript is to establish the cause of the rejection.

One of the reasons a manuscript can be rejected is that the content of the paper may not fit the scope of the journal (Chapman and Slade 2015).

The mismatch between the paper and the journal's scope and aims can occur when the paper is too specialized or when its focus falls outside the focus of the journal (Chapman and Slade 2015). Another reason that can lead to the rejection of a manuscript is the presence of clear and obvious flaws in the science.

Further, poor language or structure can also result in the rejection of the manuscript by the editor (Ali 2010). However, a manuscript can sometimes be rejected by high-ranking journals even if the reviews were (mostly) positive.

If the editor rejects the manuscript before submitting it to referees, revise it and submit it to a more appropriate journal. If the paper was submitted to referees, consider their comments, but remember that you need to preserve the story line. If the manuscript was rejected but the editor's comments suggest you should revise and resubmit, then consider making the necessary revision without altering the main message (Ali 2010).

Sometimes the rejection can occur as a result of the referees not understanding the paper enough to appreciate it. Rejection can also occur because of unclear recommendations from the referee to the editor. In such cases, one can appeal to the editor. However, exercise caution when appealing because there is a high chance of a negative response.

The best option following rejection is to revise and submit to a new journal. However, if you choose to resubmit to the same journal, write a letter to the editor explaining the improvements made and why you think the paper should be reconsidered (Ali 2010; Chapman and Slade 2015).

Researchers should also consider duplicate and prior publications. A manuscript is considered a duplicate publication if its content overlaps substantially with an already published article that the author of the manuscript has not clearly and visibly referenced (International Committee of Medical Journal Editors 2016). Prior publication, on the other hand, is a manuscript that contains information that has been released to the public domain.

Students need to ensure their manuscripts are original. However, for the already publicly available material, the writer needs to provide a clear acknowledgement of such. Without proper acknowledgment, the manuscript runs the risk of being rejected.

Therefore, to avoid the misuse of resources (i.e., time and money) on manuscripts that would be rejected, authors need to ensure that their work is original.

In addition, duplicate publications and the submission of prior publications are violations of international copyright laws and ethical conduct that should be avoided (International Committee of Medical Journal Editors 2016).

To avoid conflict with the editor, referees, and the readership, the author needs to fully acknowledge the extensive use of already published material. The letter of submission submitted by the author alongside the manuscript should indicate that the manuscript has reported work that has already been reported in large part in a published article or has been submitted for publication elsewhere. It is also the author's responsibility to provide the editor with copies of relevant material to assist the editor and referees in handling the submission.

At this point, researchers should be cautious about the material they choose to present at a scientific meeting. Although the presentation of part of the findings in scientific meetings in the form of posters or abstracts does not necessarily prevent the manuscript from being published, the provision of extensive data can cause you problems during publishing. Thus, it is good practice to avoid presenting tables or figures that will be included in the manuscript.

It is also important for researchers to consider how the dissemination of material that is presented at scientific meetings or conferences might affect the assigning of priority to the manuscript by journal editors.

Researchers should take responsibility for the preprint versions of the work. The researchers need to inform the editor about the reprints and provide the editor with copies of the preprint versions of the work.

Once published, the authors need to amend the preprint versions to ensure the readers are directed to the final published article.

It should be noted that sometimes a duplicate publication can be published without being identified by the editor. Such a duplicate publication warrants retraction with or without the author's explanation or approval (International Committee of Medical Journal Editors 2016).

In some cases, researchers may be faced with the dilemma of whether to immediately share with the public the results on critical issues that might result in saving lives or wait until the work is published. The authors with such crucial data (e.g., public health emergency data) may want to release the data immediately but do not want to risk the manuscript being considered for prior publication (International Committee of Medical Journal Editors 2016).

It is good practice to identify journals that recognize and prioritize the best interests of public health. Such editors are likely to publish the manuscript even if the results have been made public.

CHAPTER 12

Time-Saving Tools and Strategies

Researchers should be able to manage their time effectively. They must possess strong organizational abilities and plan effectively and carry out their ideas precisely.

For students, preparing and publishing research to satisfy academic requirements is a difficult task that demands excellent time management. If an appropriate method of managing the research work is not created, the research interests and other academic responsibilities may result in insufficient time for study.

Thus, this chapter offers advice and rules for the most efficient management of the research process to maximize available time. Several points are covered including the following:

- Time-planning strategies
- Time management tools used in research

Time-Planning Strategies

Plan and Begin Early

You will best hone your research skills through practice and experience. Therefore, it is likely that your first research could be the longest because there will be starts and stops along the way. You will need to read extensively to equip yourself with the knowledge that will help you troubleshoot possible problems and better develop your plan of action.

One of the most common mistakes students make is the failure to invest adequate time in extensive reading. They simply immerse themselves into the research, only to encounter problems they would have easily avoided by developing their knowledge in the area of interest.

Set Realistic and Attainable Goals

To effectively manage your time, it is ideal for establishing quantifiable, realistic, and achievable objectives within the constraints of available resources and time. Creating intermediate and immediate tasks that move you toward achieving long-term objectives may assist you in setting more realistic goals.

Additionally, you should attach quantifiable goals to a specified time constraint. Develop the practice of evaluating specified objectives regularly to ascertain accomplishment rates and potential roadblocks.

Students are encouraged to create progress reports in academic research to highlight their accomplishments and plans.

Optimize Realistic Planning

The process of optimizing realistic planning involves the fragmentation of tasks by creating to-do lists and checking off tasks as they are completed.

Complex activities should also be broken down into manageable portions with defined deadlines.

For example, when writing the manuscript, researchers are advised to spread out the writing process over a given timeline, where the completion of each section is assigned a specific time limit. It is also advisable for researchers to amass resources (i.e., knowledge, money, and research tools) before starting the research. Always seek to automate the processes as much as possible.

Prioritize Your Research

Research activities often compete with other activities for the attention of the researcher. It is the researcher's responsibility to acknowledge the importance of their work. You should also complete the objective based on the order of priority. Researchers need to effectively schedule the research work during the week that has the fewest interruptions. One should also plan a research sabbatical, which is dedicated to the completion of the research tasks.

Manage the Potential Distractions

Create an atmosphere conducive to study that is devoid of external distractions. For example, distraction-free study environments may be created by shutting off visual (such as television) and aural disturbances (such as any disruptive noise). In addition, it is critical to conduct an honest assessment of possible impediments to achieving the study goals.

Further, researchers should aim for a healthy lifestyle, including enough rest and frequent physical activity. Additionally, researchers should avoid multitasking, resulting in undesirable distractions and not boosting efficiency.

Finally, whenever feasible, the researcher should enlist the assistance of a team to complete the study work. The team may include supervisors and technical personnel who assist in the statistical analysis of collected data or people.

Look Out for Time Drains

Researchers need to guard against procrastination, interruptions, and a lack of discipline, which constitute a poor time management loop among researchers. Procrastination involves the postponement of a high-priority task in favor of a low-priority activity.

Procrastination, which manifests among researchers when they decide to attend to interruptions (low-priority activities), is caused by a lack of self-discipline.

Novices and even established researchers who are not self-disciplined can fall into the trap of attending to interruptions, which is evident by the cessation of a goal-directed activity in favor of self-gratifying activities. Attending to interruptions leads to low productivity that is manifested by the inability to meet set targets or poor-quality products as a result of last-minute rushes.

Most novice researchers who procrastinate usually console themselves by suggesting that they work best under pressure and therefore gladly indulge themselves in low-priority activities.

However, seasoned researchers know too well that high-quality research work and manuscripts require a lot of time. Research is usually a back-and-forth activity that requires researchers to regularly look back and improve on the previous steps as more and more knowledge is gained.

Some of the sources of interruptions that researchers need to guard against include email, phone calls, texts or instant messages, and visits from coworkers.

For researchers to avoid procrastinating, interruptions, and a lack of discipline, they need to honestly monitor how they use their time and identify possible causes of procrastination.

Researchers also need to prioritize their work and plan adequately. They can also delegate low-priority activities so they can focus more on the high-priority activities.

Time Management Tools Used in Research

The tools that are presented in this section will help the researcher in the development of the research idea, referencing, and documentation of the important information during research.

Table 19 provides a summary of the common tools along with the common use.

Table 19

Example of the Commonly Used Tools in Research

Tools	Links	Use
Evernote	https://evernote.com	Note taking, organizing, task lists, and archiving
OneNote	https://www.onenote.com/hrd	Information gathering and multiuser collaboration, notes sharing
CmapTools	https://cmap.ihmc.us/cmaptools/cmaptools-download/	Concept mapping software that allows the creation of graphical nodes representing concepts, as well as the connection of the nodes using lines and linking words to form a network of interrelated propositions
Freeplane	https://sourceforge.net/projects/freeplane/	Creation of mind maps and electronic outlines
MindMeister	https://www.mind-meister.com	Online mind mapping application that facilitates the visualization, sharing, and presentation of thoughts via the cloud
Bookends	https://www.sonnysoftware.com	Management of bibliographies and references when writing essays and articles

EndNote	https://endnote.com	Management of bibliographies and references for writing essays and articles
Mendeley	https://www.mendeley.com/?interaction_required=true	A reference manager that facilitates the management and sharing of research papers and generation of bibliographies for published articles
RefWorks	https://refworks.pro-quest.com	Management of bibliographies and references when writing essays and articles
Dropbox	https://www.dropbox.com	File hosting service that reduces busywork within the workspace
Google Drive	https://www.google.com/drive/	File storage and synchronization
Grammarly	http://www.grammarly.com	Digital writing tool assisting writing grammatical correct articles; also helps in the detection of plagiarism
Publisher	https://products.office.com/en-us/publisher	Useful in the designing the layout of the research article

Links to Important Critical Appraisal Worksheets

1. Systematic Reviews Critical Appraisal Sheet: https://casp-uk.net/wp-content/uploads/2018/03/CASP-Systematic-Review-Checklist-2018_fillable-form.pdf

2. Diagnostics Critical Appraisal Sheet: https://casp-uk.net/wp-content/uploads/2018/03/CASP-Diagnostic-Checklist-2018_fillable_form.pdf

3. Randomized Controlled Trials (RCT) Critical Appraisal Sheet: https://casp-uk.net/wp-content/uploads/2018/03/CASP-Randomised-Controlled-Trial-Checklist-2018_fillable_form.pdf

4. Critical Appraisal of Qualitative Studies Sheet: https://casp-uk.net/wp-content/uploads/2018/03/CASP-Qualitative-Checklist-2018_fillable_form.pdf

APPENDIX II

PRISMA Chart

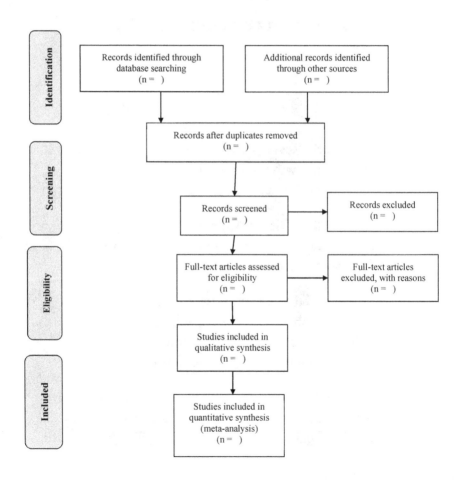

REFERENCES

Adom, D., S. Adu-Gyamfi, K. Agyekum, J. Ayarkwa, P. Dwumah, K. Abass, and W. Obeng-Denteh. 2016. "Theoretical and Conceptual Framework: Mandatory Ingredients of a Quality Research." *Journal of Education and Human Development* 5(3): 158–172.

Agee, J. 2009. "Developing Qualitative Research Questions: A Reflective Process." *International Journal of Qualitative Studies in Education* 22(4): 431–447.

Akintoye, A. 2015. "Developing Theoretical and Conceptual Frameworks." Retrieved from Jedm.oauife.edu. ng>uploads>2017/03/07.

Ali, J. 2010. Manuscript Rejection: Causes and Remedies. *Journal of Young Pharmacists* 2(1): 3.

Anderson, M., I. Solarin, S. Gerver, G. Elam, E. MacFarlane, K. Fenton, and P. Easterbrook. 2009. "Research Note: The LIVITY Study: Research Challenges and Strategies for Engaging with the Black Caribbean Community in a Study of HIV Infection." *International Journal of Social Research Methodology* 12(3): 197–209.

Baron, M. A. 2008. "Guidelines for Writing Research Proposals and Dissertations." *Division of Educational Administration: University of South Dakota*: 1–52.

Bavdekar, S. B. 2016. "Formulating the Right Title for a Research." *Journal of the Association of Physicians of India* 64: 53.

Bonevski, B., M. Randell, C. Paul, K. Chapman, L. Twyman, J. Bryant, and C. Hughes. 2014. "Reaching the Hard-to-Reach: A Systematic Review of Strategies for Improving Health and Medical Research with Socially Disadvantaged Groups." *BMC Medical Research Methodology* 14(1): 42.

Brizay, U., L. Golob, J. Globerman, D. Gogolishvili, M. Bird, B. Rios-Ellis, and S. Heidari. 2015. "Community-Academic Partnerships in HIV-Related Research: A Systematic Literature Review of Theory and Practice." *Journal of the International AIDS Society* 18(1): 19354.

Caelli, K., L. Ray, and J. Mill. 2003. "'Clear as Mud': Toward Greater Clarity in Generic Qualitative Research." *International Journal of Qualitative Methods* 2(2): 1–13.

Chapman, C., and T. Slade. 2015. "Rejection of Rejection: A Novel Approach to Overcoming Barriers to Publication." *British Medical Journal* 351: h6326.

Churchill, H., and T. Sanders. 2007. *Getting Your PhD: A Practical Insider's Guide*. Los Angeles: Sage Publications.

Cone, J. D., and S. L. Foster. 1993. *Dissertations and Theses from Start to Finish: Psychology and Related Fields*. Washington DC: American Psychological Association.

Creswell, J. W., and J. D. Creswell. 2017. *Research Design: Qualitative, Quantitative, and Mixed Methods Approaches*. Los Angeles: Sage Publications.

Cronin, P., F. Ryan, and M. Coughlan. 2008. "Undertaking a Literature Review: A Step-By-Step Approach." *British Journal of Nursing* 17(1): 38–43.

Cummings, P., and F. P. Rivara. 2002. "Responding to Reviewers' Comments on Submitted Articles." *Archives of Pediatrics and Adolescent Medicine* 156(2): 105–107.

Day, N. E. 2011. "The Silent Majority: Manuscript Rejection and Its Impact on Scholars." *Academy of Management Learning and Education* 10(4): 704–718.

Dickson-Swift, V., E. L. James, S. Kippen, and P. Liamputtong. 2007. "Doing Sensitive Research: What Challenges Do Qualitative Researchers Face?" *Qualitative Research* 7(3): 327–353.

Dine, C. J., W. C. McGaghie, G. Bordage, and J. A. Shea. 2015. "Problem Statement, Conceptual Framework, and Research Question." *Review Criteria for Research Manuscripts*: 19–25.

Dougherty, M. C., M. C. Freda, M. H. Kearney, J. G. Baggs, and M. Broome. 2011. "Online Survey of Nursing Journal Peer Reviewers: Indicators of Quality in Manuscripts." *Western Journal of Nursing Research* 33(4): 506–521.

Eakin, E. G., S. S. Bull, K. Riley, M. M. Reeves, S. Gutierrez, and P. McLaughlin. 2006. "Recruitment and Retention of Latinos in a Primary Care-Based Physical Activity and Diet Trial: The Resources for Health Study." *Health Education Research* 22(3): 361–371.

Evans, M. 2007. "Recent Research (2000–2006) Into Applied Linguistics and Language Teaching with Specific Reference to L2 French." *Language Teaching* 40(3): 211–230.

Fah, T. S., and A. F. A. Aziz. 2006. "How to Present Research Data." *Malaysian Family Physician* 1(2–3): 82.

Flamez, B., A. S. Lenz, R. S. Balkin, and R. L. Smith. 2017. *A Counselor's Guide to the Dissertation Process: Where to Start and How to Finish.* Hoboken, NJ: John Wiley and Sons.

Flory, J., and E. Emanuel. 2004. "Interventions to Improve Research Participants' Understanding in Informed Consent for Research: A Systematic Review." *Journal of the American Medical Association* 292(13): 1593–1601.

Fulton, S., and B. Krainovich-Miller. 2010. "Gathering and Appraising the Literature." *Nursing Research: Methods, Critical Appraisal and Utilization*: 56–80.

García, J. A., R. Rodriguez-Sánchez, and J. Fdez-Valdivia. 2014. "The Selection of High-Quality Manuscripts." *Scientometri cs* 98(1): 299–313.

Grange, R. I. 1998. "Saving Time, Effort and Tears: A Guide to Presenting Results." *British Journal of Urology* 81(2): 335.

Guyatt, G. H., and R. B. Haynes. 2006. "Preparing Reports for Publication and Responding to Reviewers' Comments." *Journal of Clinical Epidemiology* 59(9): 900.

Habibzadeh, F., and M. Yadollahie. 2010. "Are Shorter Article Titles More Attractive for Citations? A Crosssectional Study of 22 Scientific Journals." *Croatian Medical Journal* 51(2): 165–170.

Hart, C. 2018. *Doing a Literature Review: Releasing the Research Imagination*. Los Angeles: Sage Publications.

Hartley, J. 2012. "Titles Are the Hardest Thing: How Can We Make Them More Effective?" *Impact of Social Sciences Blog*. Retrieved from http://eprints.lse.ac.uk/51997/1/blogs.lse. ac.uk-Titles_are_the_hardest_thing_How_can_we_make_ them_more_effective.pdf.

Hergenrather, K. C., Rhodes, S. D., Cowan, C. A., G. Bardhoshi, and S. Pula. 2009. "Photovoice as Community-Based Participatory Research: A Qualitative Review." *American Journal of Health Behavior* 33(6): 686–698.

Hing, N., H. Breen, and A. Gordon. 2010. "Respecting Cultural Values: Conducting a Gambling Survey in an Australian Indigenous Community." *Australian and New Zealand Journal of Public Health* 34(6): 547–553.

Hoppitt, T., S. Shah, P. Bradburn, P. Gill, M. Calvert, H. Pall, and C. Sackley. 2012. "Reaching the 'Hard to Reach': Strategies to Recruit Black and Minority Ethnic Service Users with Rare Long-Term Neurological Conditions." *International Journal of Social Research Methodology* 15(6): 485–495.

Huston, P., and B. C. K. Choi. 2017. "Scientific Writing: A Guide to Publishing Scientific Research in the Health Sciences." *Canada Communicable Disease Report* 43(9): 169.

International Committee of Medical Journal Editors. 2016. "Recommendations for the Conduct, Reporting, Editing, and Publication of Scholarly Work in Medical Journals." Retrieved from http://www.medicc.org/mediccreview/documents/ICMJE.PDF.

Kalyanasundaram, M., S. B. Abraham, D. Ramachandran, V. Jayaseelan, J. Bazroy, Z. Singh, and A. J. Purty. 2017. "Effectiveness of Mind Mapping Technique in Information Retrieval among Medical College Students in Puducherry: A Pilot Study." *Indian Journal of Community Medicine* 42(1): 19–23.

Katz, M. J. 2009. *From Research to Manuscript: A Guide to Scientific Writing.* Berlin: Springer Science and Business Media.

Kennedy-Clark, S. 2013. "Research by Design: Design-Based Research and the Higher Degree Research Student." *Journal of Learning Design* 6(2): 26–32.

Keyzer, J. F., J. Melnikow, M. Kuppermann, S. Birch, C. Kuenneth, J. Nuovo, and M. Rooney. 2005. "Recruitment Strategies for Minority Participation: Challenges and Cost Lessons from the POWER Interview." *Ethnicity and Disease* 15(3): 395–406.

Kumar, M. J. 2013. "Editorial Commentary: Making your Research Paper Discoverable: Title Plays the Winning Trick." *IETE Technical Review* 30(5): 361–363.

Kumar, P. M., N. S. Priya, S. V. V. S. Musalaiah, and M. Nagasree. 2014. "Knowing and Avoiding Plagiarism during Scientific Writing." *Annals of Medical and Health Sciences Research* 4(3): 193–198.

Latham, J. 2017. Conceptual Framework. Retrieved from http://johnlatham.me/frameworks/research- methods-framework/conceptual-framework/

LoBiondo-Wood, G., and J. Haber. 2014. *Nursing Research-E-Book: Methods and Critical Appraisal for Evidence-Based Practice.* Elsevier Health Sciences.

McKercher, B., R. Law, K. Weber, H. Song, and C. Hsu. 2007. "Why Referees Reject Manuscripts." *Journal of Hospitality and Tourism Research* 31(4): 455–470.

McMillan, B., J. M. Green, M. W. Woolridge, L. Dyson, M. J. Renfrew, and G. P. Clarke. 2009. "Studying the Infant Feeding Intentions of Pregnant Women Experiencing Material Deprivation: Methodology of the Looking at Infant Feeding Today (LIFT) Study." *Social Science and Medicine* 68(5): 845–849.

Messuri, K. 2015. "Clarity in Medical Writing." *The Southwest Respiratory and Critical Care Chronicles* 3(12): 56–58.

Neale, J., and R. West. 2015. *Guidance for Reporting Qualitative Manuscripts.* Retrieved from https://psycnet.apa.org/record/2015-11906-002.

Okpala, P. 2018. "Assessment of the Influence of Technology on the Cost of Healthcare Service and Patient's Satisfaction." *International Journal of Healthcare Management* 11(4): 351–355.

Oliver, M. 2011. *Editorial Perspective: Writing Qualitative Manuscripts.* Retrieved from https://www.txca.org/images/tca/Documents/Journal/Journal.Winter%20Spring%20 2011.FINAL.pdf#page=9.

Osanloo, A., and C. Grant. 2016. "Understanding, Selecting, and Integrating a Theoretical Framework in Dissertation Research: Creating the Blueprint for Your 'House.'" *Administrative Issues Journal: Connecting Education, Practice, and Research* 4(2): 7.

Peregrin, T. 2007. "How to Cope with Manuscript Rejection." *Journal of the American Dietetic Association* 107(2): 190–193.

Pierson, D. J. 2004. "The Top 10 Reasons Why Manuscripts Are Not Accepted for Publication." *Respiratory Care* 49(10): 1246–1252.

Polit, D. F., and C. T. Beck. 2004. *Nursing Research: Principles and Methods.* Lippincott Williams and Wilkins.

Randolph, J. J. 2009. "A Guide to Writing the Dissertation Literature Review." *Practical Assessment, Research and Evaluation* 14(13): 1–13.

Ransohoff, D. F., and C. A. Lang. 1997. "Clinical Guideline: Part II: Screening for Colorectal Cancer with the Fecal Occult Blood Test: A Background Paper." *Annals of Internal Medicine* 126(10): 811–822.

Rezvani, A., A. Chang, A. Wiewiora, N. M. Ashkanasy, P. J. Jordan, and R. Zolin. 2016. "Manager Emotional Intelligence and Project Success: The Mediating Role of Job Satisfaction and Trust." *International Journal of Project Management* 34(7), 1112–1122.

Rimando, M., A. M. Brace, A. Namageyo-Funa, T. L. Parr, D. A. Sealy, T. L. Davis, and R. W. Christiana. 2015. "Data Collection Challenges and Recommendations for Early Career Researchers." *The Qualitative Report* 20(12): 2025–2036.

Roig, M. 2006. Avoiding Plagiarism, Self-Plagiarism, and Other Questionable Writing Practices: A Guide to Ethical Writing. Retrieved from https://bsc.ua.edu/wp-content/uploads/2017/07/plagiarism-1.pdf.

Ryan, L., E. Kofman, and P. Aaron. 2011. "Insiders and Outsiders: Working with Peer Researchers in Researching Muslim Communities." *International Journal of Social Research Methodology* 14(1): 49–60.

Saah, A. A., and C. K. Osei. 2010. "A Guideline for Choosing a Working Title for a Research Project at the Tertiary Education Level." *Journal Academica* 1(1): 24–28.

Saleem, H. 2015. "The Impact of Leadership Styles on Job Satisfaction and Mediating Role of Perceived Organizational Politics." *Procedia-Social and Behavioral Sciences* 172: 563–569.

Shebl, F., C. F. Poppell, M. Zhan, D. M. Dwyer, A. B. Hopkins, C. Groves, and E. K. Steinberger. 2009. "Measuring Health Behaviors and Landline Telephones: Potential Coverage

Bias in a Low-Income, Rural Population." *Public Health Reports* 124(4): 495–502.

Simon, M. K., and J Goes. 2011. "Developing a Theoretical Framework." Seattle, WA: Dissertation Success, LLC.

Staggers, N., and J. W. Blaz. 2013. "Research on Nursing Handoffs for Medical and Surgical Settings: An Integrative Review." *Journal of Advanced Nursing* 69(2): 247–262.

Testa, J. 2009. "The Thomson Reuters Journal Selection Process." *Transnational Corporations Review* 1(4): 59–66.

Wajdi, M., I. M. Sumartana, and N. P. D. Hudiananingsih. 2018. "Avoiding Plagiarism in Writing a Research Paper." *Soshum: Jurnal Sosial dan Humaniora [Journal of Social Sciences and Humanities]* 8(1): 94–102.

Wentz, E. A. 2013. *How to Design, Write, and Present a Successful Dissertation Proposal.* Los Angeles: Sage Publications.

Young, M. 2002. *The Technical Writer's Handbook: Writing with Style and Clarity.* Sausalito, CA: University Science Books.

CPSIA information can be obtained
at www.ICGtesting.com
Printed in the USA
LVHW102011160822
726096LV00004B/509

9 781648 959554